COOKING IN DOOR COUNTY

Other books by Pauli Wanderer

The Bittersweet Winter

The Secret at Death's Door

Dream Girl at Mystery Lake

COOKING IN DOOR COUNTY

SECOND EDITION

By Pauli Wanderer

Illustrations by
Karmen Effenberger-Thompson

Wm Caxton Ltd
Ellison Bay, Wisconsin
1996

Published by:

> WM Caxton Ltd
> 12037 Highway 42
> Ellison Bay, WI 54210
>
> (414) 854-2955

Copyright 1985, 1996 by Pauline Wesley Wanderer.
Illustrations by Karmen Effenberger-Thompson.

All rights reserved. No part of this book may be reproduced in any form or by any means without written permission from the publisher, except by a reviewer, who may quote brief passages in a review.

Printed in the United States of America.

10 9 8 7 6 5 4 3 2 1

This book is printed on acid-neutral paper bound in sewn signatures and is intended to provide a very long useful life.

ISBN 0-940473-35-6 (Original paperback)

In memory of Justine Aynsley.

TABLE OF CONTENTS

INTRODUCTION TO THE SECOND EDITION
INTRODUCTION TO THE FIRST EDITION

WATER AND SHORE 13

John Wesley's Pan-Fried Trout *15*
Trout with Bacon Blanket *16*
Door County Rainbows on the Grill *16*
Poached Trout *17*
Cooking Trout in Bouillon *17*
Grilled Salmon or Lake Trout *18*
One Way to Stuff a Fish *18*
Rainy Day Fish Chowder *19*
Favorite Fish Soup *20*
Whitefish for Purists *21*
Whitefish Liver Pâté *22*
Kitchen Fish Boil *24*
Boiling Fish Outdoors *26*
Coleslaw *26*
Swedish-Style Boiled Salmon *27*
Bay Crabs *28*
Shipboard Curry *30*
Quick Chutney *30*
Sailor's Shepherd Pie *30*
First-Night Fillets *31*
Desserts under Sail *31*
Aynsley's English Tea in a Hamper *32*
Cress Sandwiches *33*
Rowley's Bay Scones *33*
Roasted Chicken with Mustard *34*
Cucumber Sandwiches *35*
Mud Lake Mallards *37*
Coot Stew from Mud Lake *37*
Partridge in a Pot *38*
Wild Goose and Red Cabbage *38*
Venison Pot Roast *39*
Woodcock Stuffed with Lingonberries *39*
Wine-Baked Pheasant *40*
Wild Rice for Beginners *40*
Red Cabbage and Apples *41*
Red Cabbage Salad *41*
Crackers *44*
Anchovy-Stuffed Eggs *45*
Boiling a Whole Tongue *45*
Tongue Salad *45*
Scandinavian Yellow Pea Soup *46*
Pickled Beets *46*

WOODS AND BYWAYS 47

Morels in Butter *50*
Morels in Sour Half-and-Half *50*
Stuffed Morels *51*
Morels and Macaroni a la Crème *51*
Serendipity Oyster Fry *52*
Cuban Bread in Gills Rock *53*
Drying Chanterelles *54*
Freezing Chanterelles *55*
Chanterelle Picnic Omelet *55*
About Flour Tortillas *55*
Cream of Chanterelle Soup Supreme *56*
Dandelion Wine *57*
Wilted Dandelion Salad *57*
Greens and Eggs *57*

Steamed Fiddleheads 58
Fiddlehead Soup 58
Fiddlehead Salad 58
Fresh Tomato Sauce 60
Marinara Sauce 60
Clam Sauce with Wild Basil 61
Chair Rushing 61
Cattail Shoots 61
Stir-fried Day Lily Buds 61
Stuffed Grape Leaves 63
Stuffed Cabbage Leaves 63
Door County Asparagus 64
Hollandaise Sauce 64
Asparagus Vinaigrette 66
Asparagus Salad Supreme 66
Wild Asparagus Pie 66
Béchamel Sauce 66

Maple Grapefruit 67
Dried-Fruit Compote 68
Maple Salad Dressing 68
Maple Baked Apples 68
Maple Syrup Custards 68
Wild Raspberry Pie 69
Thimbleberry Sauce 70
Wild Strawberry Jam 70
Strawberry Leaf Tea 71
Wild Blueberry Grunt 71
Blackberry Cobbler 72
Blackberry Tonic 73
Once-a-Year Gooseberry Pie 74
Vivian's Orange Beechnut Bread 74
Beechnut Pie 76
Pasties 76

ORCHARDS AND FIELDS 77

Door County Cherry Pie 80
Cherry Tarts 80
Easy Cherry Cobbler 81
Cherry Bounce 81
Summer Cherry Soup 81
Marion's Cherry Rhubarb Dessert 82
Drying Apples 82
Suzy's Apple Crisp 83
Courtland Apple Pie 83
Door County Apple Butter 84
Apple Chutney 84
French Apple Tart 85
Country Fried Apples 85
Lazy Applesauce 85
Swedish Apple Cake 86
Vanilla Sauce 86
Apple Nut Bread 86
Apple Pastry Bars 87

Door County Cherry Bars 87
Danish Red Cabbage 88
Bounty Stew for Poor Poets and Friends 89
Easy French Bread 90
Mashed Turnips 92
Beautiful Beets 92
Pickled Cucumbers 92
Zucchini Stew 94
Zucchini and Yellowneck Salad 94
Corn or Zucchini Fritters 94
Stir-fried Zucchini 95
Fresh Tomato Soup 95
Fried Green Tomatoes 95
Julie's Lasagne 96
Tomatoes for Dessert 96
Brined Dill Pickles 96
Salmon Pie 99

Swedish Potato Salad   *99*
Smoked Salmon Tidbits   *99*
Rosettes   *100*
Progressive Barn Tour Picnic   *101*
Quick Cold Borscht   *101*
Salmon Seviche   *101*
Curried Chicken Salad   *102*
Fresh Currant Dessert   *102*
Fettuccini with Butter and Cheese   *103*
Green Chili Rellenos   *104*
French Onion Soup   *104*
Gorp   *105*
Jerky   *106*
Pemmican   *106*
Après Ski Smorgasbord   *108*
Eggs with Caviar   *108*
Bird's Nest   *108*
Good Strong Coffee   *109*
Glogg   *110*
Spritz Cookies   *110*
Joy's Danish Cookies   *110*

ROOTS   *111*

Kneecaps   *114*
Smelts Wisconsin Bar Style   *115*
Pickled Smelts   *115*
Pickled Suckers of Disputed Origin   *116*
Frog Legs with Garlic   *116*
Brussels's Belgian Tripe   *119*
Chicken Booyah Van Bellinger   *119*
Belgian Pie   *120*
Cooking Pigs' Feet   *121*
Pickled Pigs' Feet   *122*
Headcheese   *122*
Fourth of July Bratwurst   *125*
Emily's Down-Home Fried Chicken   *126*
Wild Grapevine Wreath   *129*
Tailgate Picnic Bread   *129*
Another Way to Stuff a Bread   *130*
German Fried Potatoes   *132*
Baked New Potaotes   *132*
Potato Pancakes Just Like Kaap's   *133*
Anderson Hotel Steamed Cherry Pudding   *135*
Anderson Hotel Fresh Peach Pie   *136*
Anderson Hotel Strawberry Pie   *136*
Moravian Sugar Cake   *138*
Moravian Christmas Cookies   *139*
Vivian's Pea Soup   *139*
Gravlaks   *140*
Norwegian Fruit Soup   *141*
Swedish Pancakes   *141*
Swedish Meatballs   *142*
Apples and Pears Pudding   *144*
Limpa Bread   *144*

INTRODUCTION TO THE SECOND EDITION

INTRODUCTION TO SECOND EDITION

Since *COOKING IN DOOR COUNTY* first appeared, our old house has survived several calamities, including battering storms and dry rot. Its underpinnings have been shored up once again, with hopes that it will stand another ten years. When the 1940s icebox died, we replaced it with a 1970s model (which has a separate freezer). It's the newest thing in the house. The Deco stove has resisted interment and is still a working collector's item.

The children are grown now. They've become weekenders in the county. Still, when they're here, they continue to swim, cycle, and forage with me, much as they did when they were small. They no longer spend hours searching for bay crabs down at the shore, but I suspect even that tradition will be revived when grandchildren come along. We continue to cook from the recipes found in these pages, and in that way, at least, our lives have changed very little.

As for the county itself, change is constant and unpredictable. We can no longer just stop in the middle of Highway 42 (anytime after Labor Day) to visit with a neighbor; we'd be horn-blasted off the road. Or worse.

One of Door County's glories are the early barns. Each year on arrival, I race around to see which of our favorites are still left standing. We cherish those that remain, but we're not fools about the cost of preserving these old structures, and we wish there were some way to save these relics from falling down or being torn down to make way for new construction.

Up and down the county, each summer, wide meadows and daisy fields disappear and ever more and more enormous summer "cottages" fill our eyes. The beech grove that gave us buckets of chanterelles is now a private tennis court. Our secret morel patch has gone to condominiums, and the best wild asparagus spot is now under a concrete foundation. As I write, choice pine and oak woodlands in the southern Door are threatened by state highway construction. The delicate balance that allows the native communities to exist is much more imperiled than it was only ten years ago. And all of us who know this amazing peninsula and its waters also know what must be done to protect it.

Time transforms everything, and even places and business that we think of as institutions have changed or disappeared altogether. The Viking Orchard is no longer — though the barn with its fine cupola and the house remain. The Tria Gallery, once owned by Ruth and Philip Philipon (who restored its remarkable barn), is now the Starry Night Gallery, owned by Wallace and Donna Wold. Teskie's "on-your-honor" fruit stand has become a full-blown business with its own new building. And, although Koepsels do more business than ever, I no longer see furs hanging next to the zucchini bin.

Philip and Rosemary Voight have moved on to bring new culinary life to the Lake Side Inn in Jacksonport. After a long and varied career, Bob Lapp has finally retired from his charter fishing and handyman activities, and Roy and Charlotte Lukes have retired from the Ridges, though their lifelong partnership with nature continues.

After the fire, the Hotel DuNord rose again like a phoenix, and the new building is slowly gaining patina. Grapevine wreaths have had their season in the sun, but the Red Barn still holds its summer tailgate antiques sale. The Omnibus is long gone, and the old ski area that Al Johnson, Bob Lapp and Eddie Valentine knew so well is slated to become a huge theme park, unless lovers of the delicate balance prevail in court.

We are all of us here for but a moment on this planet. My old neighbor Alvina Horskey, who mourned leaving her log house on Hedgehog Harbor, is dead. John Ellstrom is also gone, and most of his stories with him. So is Lester Newman, though the Pioneer Store remains a landmark, with Carol keeping it as it was. Hub's Motel continues to be the oldest continuing guest lodging on the peninsula — more than 100 years — though Ralph "Mickey" Hubbard is among the angels.

When Justine Aynsley wasn't canoeing up the Mink River with my daughter Julie, she could often be found jumping her horse or swimming at Europe Bay; she was killed in an auto accident here in the county shortly after her eighteenth birthday.

I must add a note on a recipe that I've taken some joshing about over the years — the one for pickled suckers. In Door County parlance, leeches are not the only "suckers." Suckers may also be large, bottom-feeding "rough" fish of the family Catostomidae; they have a thick lip that is adapted for clinging by sucking. If you catch one of these suckers, chunk and pickle it as you would smelts.

*   *   *

A special thanks to Dorothy Anderson Metzel for her sharp eye and artistic acumen in helping to prepare this second edition.

Boulder, Colorado
July 1996

INTRODUCTION TO THE FIRST EDITION

No matter where else I find myself, I'd rather be in Door County. And if I could have my proverbial cake, I'd like it to have just stopped raining.

In my mind's eye, I see the sky clearing, the bay so blue it takes the breath away, the leaves struck livid green, the magic of woods and water.

I walk through the trees to the water's edge, and I am at home. With my family, I set up cooking, cleaning, and writing in an old house, gently haunted by pioneer ghosts. The house is coming apart seam by seam; we shore up and caulk. It stands. It's home.

My roots lie across the bay. On the Fourth of July I have seen faint sparks from fireworks shot off from the shores of Menominee, where I was born. So I am, as any transplant can tell you, a foreigner.

I don't mind any more, for I'm in good company. At one time, all white men and women were foreigners in these parts. The Indians, whose hunting and fishing ground it was, have not come back to claim it.

In another way we're all here on borrowed time, keepers of the landscape and the water. For a good portion of the county is an island of extreme fragility, and its delicate balance is in peril. We don't dare treat the island as white folks treated the island of Manhattan. We know what we'd get, and it wouldn't be what we came here to find.

The essence of Door County lies beyond my most diligent efforts to describe it. When I'm at the beach, I feel it is there, that mix of water, sand, and big sky, with the woods forcing the dune's edge. To a friend, it is Ephraim's Eagle Harbor, a clutter of boats within an arm of limestone ledge. To my sister, it is a field of oxeye daisies on a back road. To a traveler I overheard once in a local grocery, it's "those damn beautiful barns," and how could he get one to take home? A cross-country skier finds it along a winter trail by the frozen Newport shore. To thousands, the county is fishing, pure and simple.

And I am back where I started. Door County defies definition. In some way, as with other islands, the county has put its stamp on food. Much is derivative of the pioneers who came and stayed to feed themselves and their families: the Norwegians, the Swedes, the Icelanders, the Germans, and the Belgians. Otherwise, the region's cookery springs from what can be harvested from land and water.

I like to eat, and if there are other eaters in the immediate vicinity, I like to cook. Feeling nostalgic for Door County in winter, I've wanted a book I could leaf through to bring back memories of trout fried within minutes of being taken off the hook, or wild raspberries picked in the rain and smothered in sour cream and maple syrup, or a supper of new potatoes, fresh sweet corn, and crayfish shared with old friends on a small, stony beach.

I played the association test with a few others. In an unofficial and casual poll I took, cherry pie, Swedish pancakes, whitefish, and boiled trout came up time after time. A few responses included Belgian pie, bratwurst, and smoked salmon.

Gathering these together with a good many of my own, I've put together another way to look at Door County. This is a private view for the most part, though I'm sure many others will find their experiences repeated here.

When I get back to the county, I will take these memories into the kitchen and share them with whomever turns up to eat the provender.

ACKNOWLEDGMENTS

I would like to give special thanks to Marge and Hal Grutzmacher, who started it all; to Nan Pirnack and Jim Johnson of the *Town and Country Review*, Boulder, Colorado, who carried so many of my Door County columns; to the good cooks Joy Paulson, Marion Metzer, Jenny Aynsley, Jackie Van Bellinger, Emily Hunter, Bobsey Thompson, Suzy Roesler, Vivian Wesley, Roger Voight, Duane Quiatt, and Julie Wanderer; to Eddie Valentine for the use of family recipes; to the anonymous duck hunter from Suamico for game recipes and much encouragment; and to my neighbors Alvina Horskey, Don Peot, Tim Weborg, Gladys and Wallace Weborg, and Yvonne Voight for much talk about old Door County days.

I would also like to thank my illustrator, Karmen Effenberger-Thompson, and my editor, Becky Knight.

WATER·AND·SHORE

Fishing fever. I grew up with a Wisconsin trout fisherman—my father. My mother was a fishing widow, and she took that for granted. When she got sick of staying home, she gathered up a year's supply of magazines and her berry pail and joined the angler.

By my father's standards, there is no real trout fishing in Door County. He was a purist in a sport of purists. No worms, no salmon eggs, no trolling. His old felt fishing hat was stuck full of his favorite dry and wet flies, his hip waders were a mass of patches, but his bamboo rod was a Leonard. He was the first to show me how to crawl to the stream bank, so as not to cast a shadow that would alert the wily trout.

My own children do not give a fig for this sort of sport. They clomp down to the docks in Gills Rock loaded with pop, tackle, and worms. They yell back and forth to each other, arguing over who's got whose rod and which one stole the worm can, and yell even louder when one of them catches an unwitting rainbow.

The one rule that carries down from their grandfather is this: You catch them, you clean them. Consequently, when our daughter was seven and caught her first fish, we put a knife in her hands and showed her how. I've seldom been caught since with a sink full of fish and a bunch of kids streaking out the door to go swimming.

Another rule of thumb which applies in our house is to leave on the head. My mother often put a caper in the eye socket if she was entertaining a squeamish guest, but generally we have presented trout at the table as they left the water.

Here's how we cook trout my father's way, plus a few variations that he never tried.

JOHN WESLEY'S PAN-FRIED TROUT

trout
peanut oil or bacon grease
fine cornmeal
salt and pepper

I use a heavy iron skillet, perhaps a number 8, for 6 or 7 pan-sized trout. Heat about a half inch of oil or grease until it is just at the smoking point. Meanwhile, dredge the trout in the cornmeal or put the meal into a paper bag and shake the trout. Pop the trout into the pan and cook 3 or 4 minutes on each side. Salt and pepper as they cook. Remove to a hot platter and serve immediately. Trout cooked fresh from the water do not require lemon, as they are a miracle of sizzling sweetness on their own.

TROUT WITH BACON BLANKET

My father would say this is gilding the lily and that no honest brook trout would stand for being smothered in all these trimmings. I reserve this recipe for trout that have been frozen.

6 rainbow trout
12 slices bacon
salt and pepper
mushrooms
salad oil
bay leaves
handful chopped parsley
2 cloves garlic

Preheat the oven to 400 degrees. Chop 5 or 6 large mushrooms very fine and mix with the pressing from 2 cloves of garlic. Salt and pepper the trout and put the garlic and mushroom mix inside each cavity. Add a half bay leaf to each and wrap the trout in bacon, 2 slices to each fish. Rub a bit of salad oil on the bottom of a baking dish. Arrange the trout within. Bake in the oven about 20 minutes or until done. Remove to a hot platter and sprinkle with parsley. Garnish with lemon slices. Boiled potatoes done in the Irish way are a good accompaniment to these dressed-up trout.

DOOR COUNTY RAINBOWS ON THE GRILL

6 trout
olive oil
carrot sticks
fennel branches or ground fennel seeds
freshly ground pepper

Start a charcoal fire and add cast-off apple trimmings or maple branches found in the woods. Salt and pepper the trout lightly. Then get your hands into about a half cup of olive oil and grease the trout liberally inside and out. Stick a few carrot sticks into the cavity of each trout and skewer it shut. If you have fennel branches, lay them on the grill and lay the trout on top. Otherwise, sprinkle fennel seeds on the trout while they are cooking. Cook a few minutes on each side and serve. (The olive oil should prevent the skins from sticking to the grill.) Serve these trout with lemon for extra zest.

POACHED TROUT

6 trout

Court bouillon:
2 cups water
2 cups dry vermouth
several slices onion
6 or 7 peppercorns
½ teaspoon salt
½ teaspoon coriander
1 stalk celery
1 bay leaf

Bring to a boil and simmer about 20 minutes. Strain.

COOKING TROUT IN BOUILLON

Pour the bouillon into a flat pan. When it comes to a boil, slip in the trout. Simmer them about 10 minutes or until the flesh of the fish flakes easily with a knife. For a large fish, use this rule of thumb: 10 minutes per pound. Trout cooked in this manner are good hot or cold. No matter how you plan to serve them, let the fish sit in the poaching liquid a few minutes so they stay juicy. Then slip to a platter and serve with lemon or a good mayonnaise.

Cover the kettle and simmer very slowly for 5 or 6 minutes. Serves 4 to 6.

The sport that's raging in Door County is big game fishing with a down rigger. Salmon and lake trout. In our neck of the woods, we can walk down to the water almost any evening in the summer at sunset and get our eyes full of big fish, either at the Shoreline, Captain Paul's, or Gary Gros's landing spot at the Weborg docks. Out come the Polaroids, the ear-splitting grins, and the weighing in.

What do you do with a big fish once you've landed it? You might take it to the Weborgs' or the Voights' to be smoked, or you could smoke it yourself.

You might prefer to fillet it and pack it home on dry ice. Or if you're staying in the county and find yourself with a 24-pound salmon, you could invite friends and just-met neighbors in for a salmon grill.

The PCBs are concentrated in the fatty tissues. The best way to get rid of them is to cook out the fat. A good hot charcoal or wood fire does this nicely.

GRILLED SALMON OR LAKE TROUT

salmon or trout
oil
salt and pepper

Put the salmon slices on the grill skin side down, first brushing them with oil so they don't stick. Literally grill out the fat before you turn them. As the fat drips into the fire, it will send up a good deal of savory smoke, which will flavor the fish when you've turned it flesh side down. The slices from a large fish may take up to 10 minutes on one side but less time on the second side, so test with a fork to make certain it's done but not dried out. Grilled lake trout or salmon may be basted with your favorite barbecue sauce.

The following recipe was an instant, intuitive effort I seized on several years back when my son Matthew and his friend Craig Rosenkranz came up the drive at sundown dragging a monster fish. I panicked, thinking of our 40-year-old icebox, which holds a few groceries and several trays of ice cubes. The closer they got, the larger the sea monster grew.

They cleaned it, lathering their clothes with blood and guts, and saved the innards for catching crawfish. The salmon, a gift from a fisherman who hated fish on a platter, was saved by the boys from a dump in the woods.

I sawed off a 6-pound chunk and turned on the oven. Then I stuffed the fish with whatever vegetables I could turn up.

ONE WAY TO STUFF A FISH

1 large chunk salmon or lake trout
zucchini
fresh tomatoes
new potatoes
onions
celery
carrots
dillweed
dry vermouth
salt and pepper
vegetable oil

Turn the oven to 375 degrees. Chop the vegetables into smallish cubes. Rub the fish lightly with oil, salt, and pepper inside and out. Sprinkle with dill. Lay the fish on a piece of foil, stuff with vegetables, and arrange the overflow around it. Just before closing the foil, pour an ample amount of dry vermouth over the fish. Place in a large pan and into the oven. Bake at least 30 minutes or until the fish flakes easily with a small, sharp knife.

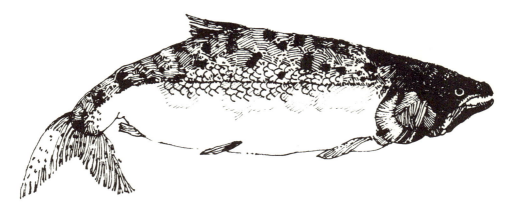

There are certain days in summer, particularly in August, when the rain drives down for hours with relentless force. These are drag-out-the-jigsaw-puzzle days or letter-writing days, according to one's tastes. The weather demands a fire in the wood stove and a big pot of soup. A jug of wine and an old-fashioned hand of pinochle will not hurt the appetite.

RAINY DAY FISH CHOWDER

2 ounces salt pork, diced fine
2 onions, chopped fine
2 cups potatoes, peeled and diced
2 pounds trout or salmon, boned and chunked
2 cups boiling water
2 cups light cream
¼ teaspoon paprika
salt and white pepper to taste

Try out the salt pork in a good-sized kettle until golden. Remove the pieces with a slotted spoon and drain. Sauté the onion in fat until limp. Stir in the potatoes; then add the fish. Pour boiling water over the fish and bring to a boil. Reduce the heat, cover, and simmer 20 minutes. Add the salt pork and paprika. Add the cream slowly, taking care it does not boil. Season with salt and pepper. Cover the kettle and simmer very slowly for 5 or 6 minutes. Serves 4 to 6.

This next recipe is my favorite fish soup. It's another of those empty-out-the-vegetable-bin inspirations; the contents, however, must be at least vaguely Mediterranean. Tomatoes in some form and garlic (never powdered!) are, with the fish stock, the core of this soup.

You shouldn't have too much trouble in Door County talking a commercial fisherman out of bones and heads from several large fish. The addition of several pounds of lake trout will clinch the flavor of this soup.

FAVORITE FISH SOUP

bones and heads from several large fish
3 pounds lake trout
2 quarts water
2 cups dry vermouth
1 teaspoon fennel seeds (scant)
4 medium-sized onions, chopped
4 cloves garlic, minced
2 green peppers, sliced
8 tablespoons olive oil
8 cups fresh tomatoes, chopped or
2 large cans of tomatoes, sliced
2 cups celery, chopped
8 medium potatoes, diced
2 to 3 cups garbanzos, cooked
1½ bay leaves
3 teaspoons salt
1 teaspoon black pepper
1 cup parsley, chopped
1 teaspoon dried basil or
1 tablespoon fresh basil, chopped

Simmer the fish heads and bones in water and wine with the fennel seeds for a half hour. Drain and reserve the broth. Pick the meat from the bones. Reserve. Don't forget the cheek, which has 2 delectable, fat morsels. Take a large, heavy frying pan and heat the olive oil. Sauté the onion and green pepper until the onion is transparent. Add the garlic at the last minute and stir about; then remove from the heat. Put the fish stock into a large, heavy pot. Add the sautéed vegetables. Add the potatoes, garbanzos, tomatoes, celery, herbs, salt, and pepper. Bring to a boil. Reduce to a simmer and cook until the potatoes are nearly done. Add the fish, which you've cut into bite-sized pieces, and simmer another 10 minutes. Correct the seasonings. Add water if the soup is too thick. This soup should feed a crowd of 10 to 16 people. Serve in heated soup bowls and pass a bowl of grated Parmesan and a basket of toasted French bread slices.

In summer, I often awake at dawn to the sound of the bird chorus and the fishing tugs leaving the harbor. Hedgehog Harbor, the old maps say. Gills Rock, for all its ferry traffic, is still primarily a fishing village, the last on the peninsula.

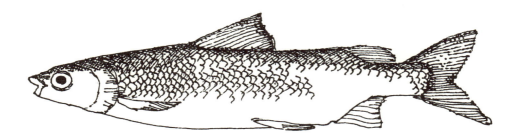

Families like the Teskies, the Voights, and the Weborgs have been engaged in fishing for generations.

The fishermen are surely as rugged as the lobstermen of Maine, about whom a good deal more has been sung and written. Lake Michigan is as fierce and wily a body of water as the Atlantic and probably more ticklish to fish, as storms come up out of nowhere in minutes.

Whitefish is king. It is never inexpensive, but always worth the price. Although restaurants have made their reputations on baked, stuffed whitefish, I believe it is best cooked in butter and sprinkled with chopped parsley.

WHITEFISH FOR PURISTS

1 pound whitefish fillet
2 to 3 tablespoons butter
2 teaspoons parsley, minced

Remove the fish skin with a very sharp knife. Dry the fish. Heat the butter in a heavy skillet. When the butter is bubbling but not yet brown, slip in the fish and cook over medium heat for about 4 minutes. Turn with care so as not to break the fish and cook another 4 or 5 minutes. Place the fish on a hot platter, pour pan juices over it, and sprinkle with parsley. Salt the fish at the table. Will serve 2 whitefish addicts nicely.

One evening a few years back, fisherman Tim Weborg appeared through the backwoods trail and offered us a pint of whitefish livers. I remembered my grandmother doleing out daily portions of cod-liver oil and surveyed this neighborly gift with some reserve. "Better than chicken livers," said Tim. "Umm," said I. "Much sweeter than chicken livers," he persisted.

I cautiously took his word for it and spent the next hour digging through old cookbooks for an appropriate recipe. Perhaps, had I been wise enough to truly believe him, I might have sautéed the livers in butter with chopped onion. Instead, I made a pâté and took it to a party, where it was devoured in minutes.

WHITEFISH LIVER PÂTÉ

2 pounds fresh whitefish livers
1 small onion, finely chopped
2 tablespoons parsley, minced
2 teaspoons black pepper
1 teaspoon powdered ginger (scant)
¼ teaspoon cinnamon
2 teaspoons salt
1 tablespoon brandy
1 tablespoon Madeira or port
bacon strips

Put the livers through the fine blade of a meat grinder twice or use a food processor. If using the old-fashioned grinder, you'll find the livers go through more easily if you sauté them a minute in a bit of butter. Mix together the livers and all the ingredients except the bacon strips. Line a loaf pan with bacon, pack in the pâté, and bake in a 350-degree oven for about 1½ hours. Remove and cool the pâté under pressure. I use another loaf pan filled with canned goods or bricks. Chill the pâté before serving. Serve with melba toast or country bread. 12 modest servings.

I've eaten smoked fish in New York, London, and Dublin, all of it lovely. Still, I believe the best comes from the Voights' or Weborgs' smokehouses in Gills Rock. The maple smoke and a master's skill after years of experience accounts for this sweet succulence.

At some point I thought about smoking my own, and to that end had dragged onto the property an old refrigerator. Someone had told me it would make an ideal smoker. After reading up on the subject, however, I decided to leave smoking fish to the experts. Anything I might produce would be of strikingly inferior quality to what was being done around the corner.

For others who might like to try smoking fish, I'd suggest buying a copy of *Getting the Most from Your Great Lakes Salmon*, by Johnson, Stuiber, and Lindsay, put out as a public information report by the University of Wisconsin Sea Grant College Program. This book offers practical advice on skinning, canning, smoking, and otherwise dealing with salmon.

Fish houses in the area will smoke the fish you've caught. A word of caution: Fish is lightly smoked here and does not travel well without careful refrigeration. If you have a long way to travel, perhaps you could talk the smoker into giving your prize fish a deeper, drier smoking than is the rule.

The beginnings of the fish boil in Door County lie with the fishermen themselves, who boiled some of their catch on board the fishing tugs. As tourism grew in the county, they sometimes hired themselves out to fix boils for private parties. Local churches took up the idea and helped plant the tradition. Soon restaurants began to set aside an evening for an outdoor boil: The Viking in Ellison Bay, the Edgewater in Ephraim, and the White Gull Inn in Fish Creek led the rest. Nowadays, one could eat boiled fish every night for several weeks at a different restaurant throughout the peninsula.

The fanfare of the caldron boiling over when the fire is stoked high is the trademark of the outside boil. The theory is that this clinches the flavor of the fish and drives out the fat. Nonetheless, I've eaten boiled trout done in the kitchen that tastes to me every bit as good.

Now that I've set down this heresy, here's a recipe to use on your own kitchen stove. If the kettle boils over, leaving a mess, something's gone wrong.

KITCHEN FISH BOIL

For each person:
½ pound lake trout or whitefish, cleaned and chunked
2 small onions, peeled
3 small new potatoes
¼ cup salt (scant)
cheesecloth
butter

Take a large canning or fish kettle and fill half full of water. Add the salt. Use the noniodized type or use sea salt. Bring the water and salt to a stiff boil. Add the potatoes and boil 10 minutes. Add the onions and boil 8 minutes. Wrap the fish in cheesecloth and boil 15 minutes. Drain. Arrange on a platter and serve with lots of melted Wisconsin butter. Margarine will not do.

Any of us lucky enough to own one of those large iron caldrons (sometimes seen retired as petunia gardens) can stage a fish boil for a big crowd. *Stage* is the proper verb, for the event is dramatic.

The traditional menu for a boil includes fish, potatoes, onions, rye bread, coleslaw, and cherry pie. Cherry cobbler has been snuck in as an alternative.

Searching for a big boil recipe, I caught Captain Roger Voight as he was about to take out a crowd of hopeful fishermen and women aboard his Lucky Lady II

in Gills Rock. Roger Voight grew up around some professionals: his mother, Yvonne, who ran boils at the Shoreline, and Phil and Rosemary Voight, now at the Viking. Roger does occasional fish boils for large crowds when he can work it into his heavy fishing schedule.

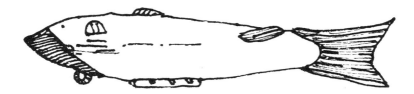

BOILING FISH OUTDOORS

1 cup salt to each 3 gallons water

For each person:
several new potatoes
several small onions
1 pound fish, lake trout or whitefish

Chunk the fish into half-pound steaks. Chop the ends off the potatoes and scrub. Peel the onions. Get the salted water to boiling in a large caldron. Drop in the potatoes. Build up the fire. Boil the potatoes for 10 minutes. Add the onions. Build up the fire. Boil 7 minutes. Build up the fire. Add the fish when the water is boiling strong again. Boil 9 minutes. Stoke up the fire again and boil the broth over. Drain the vegetables and fish. Serve right away with lots of melted butter.

There are probably as many coleslaw recipes as there are cooks. Here's an old-timer that uses an uncooked egg in the dressing.

COLESLAW

1 large cabbage
1½ cups mild vinegar
1 egg
1 tablespoon butter
1 tablespoon sugar
salt and white pepper

Peel off the outer leaves of the cabbage and shred very fine with a sharp French knife or a slaw cutter. Lay the cabbage in a bowl, sprinkling with a little salt and pepper as you do so. Heat the vinegar to a boil. Beat the egg well, add a bit of hot vinegar to the egg, and pour the egg into the hot vinegar in a steady stream, beating all the while. Add the sugar and butter, beating constantly. Mix the dressing into the slaw and set to cool. 8 to 10 servings.

A recipe for limpa bread is found on page 144 and one for cherry pie on page 80.

Here is a traditional Swedish recipe for boiling salmon. Because it is simmered gently, it might better be called poached. Such a classy word, *poached*, which, at least for me, conjures up fish houses on the eastern seaboard, fancied up with nautical antiques. This recipe, however, could not be simpler, and it ought to be a good one for a novice cook.

SWEDISH-STYLE BOILED SALMON

4½- to 6-pound salmon
4 tablespoons vinegar
2 sprigs dill
12 whole peppercorns
1 small onion, sliced
1 bay leaf
4 teaspoons salt
cheesecloth

Discard the head and tail of a cleaned salmon. Bring water to boil in a large kettle and add the seasonings. Boil for a few minutes while you wrap the fish. Lay the fish in the water gently. The water should just cover the fish. Bring the water back to a boil and then simmer the salmon for about 30 minutes. Lift the fish out and lay on a rack to drain. Remove the cheesecloth. Slide the salmon to a handsome platter and garnish with dill. Serve immediately with melted butter mixed with lemon juice or with your best hollandaise sauce. Serves 6.

Before my children properly learned how to fish, they busied themselves by hunting crayfish. (*Bay crabs*, Wisconsin natives call them, and *crawdads* to southerners.) There may be as many methods to catching them as there are devotees of the sport. One of the more astonishing methods, preferred by Oregonians, is to take a large umbrella and some raw hamburger to a tidal river and wait for the crayfish to crawl in and begin their feast. Then snap goes the umbrella, and you take home supper.

Another method, favored by most children I know, is to go in the water, turn over stones, and grab the crayfish with bare hands. A pail in attendance is a must, as these fellows do not sit by waiting for the journey home.

If you plan to cook and eat them, it is wise to set aside a dozen for each person at the table. The meat is sweet, but there is very little of it, and one continues to build an appetite while digging out the morsels.

Any French cookbook can supply recipes for crayfish dressed up in the most elegant fashion. Our family prefers them, stateside at least, boiled and served with melted butter or a good mayonnaise.

Although I've read the British Anti-vivisectionist League's views on boiling lobsters alive and the pain inflicted by that cruel method, I find it impossible to sever the cranial nerves of five or six dozen crayfish. Here's how I kill them, though, I admit, with a faint heart.

BAY CRABS

several dozen crayfish freshly caught
jelly kettle ⅔ full of water
1 large bay leaf
1 onion, sliced
1 carrot, sliced
8 peppercorns
2 teaspoons salt

Cover the kettle and bring all the ingredients except the crayfish to a boil. Simmer the stock for about 15 minutes. Bring back to a fierce, rolling boil and push in about 2 dozen crayfish at a time; cook them 5 or 6 minutes, until they turn bright red. Remove with a slotted spoon. Bring the stock to a boil again and repeat. Serve bay crabs with nutcrackers and pickers, large napkins, and a big pot of melted butter.

From a landlubber's point of view, to see this county by water is to turn the world inside out. A lighthouse viewed by sea is surely not the same building as that come across by land. Nor is the church steeple seen from beyond the harbor.

Being landlocked now, except for a small and unadventuresome canoe, I think back to a sailing trip around Death's Door, made in my college days with some old chums on a fine wooden boat named *Flying Swan*. We boarded in Sturgeon Bay and sailed north past the Cowles's splendid Horseshoe Farms to Fish Creek. Putting in there and taking on ice and groceries, I recall looking at native and tourist alike and thinking, Poor souls, they're landlocked. We were on our second day, getting our sea legs, and had come to stare and then disappear over a watery horizon.

I might be forgiven, as this was not snobbery. I was nineteen and wildly romantic, full of poetry and notions about sailing alone around the world, filling a log book with sonnets as I battled the big water. That summer Lake Michigan *was* the sea, and sailing into the wind was like flying. Our life aboard the boat—hauling sail, polishing brass, skinny-dipping at midnight, and running up the cocktail flag at five as if we were legal age to drink—filled me with a fierce sense of power.

Ship's stores on that journey up and through Death's Door were a general assortment of youthful treats: bratwurst, hamburger, pickles, chips, beer, Rainbow bread, and sweet rolls. If I were to have another chance at it, I'd only change the menu.

Following are some ideas for interesting shipboard cookery to be used on a voyage when you don't want to put into port frequently to take on supplies. These recipes came from Emily Hunter, who sailed to Tahiti with her family on a 37-foot ketch. They work as well for Lake Michigan sailors readying themselves to sail around the world and back again.

SHIPBOARD CURRY

canned beef chunks in gravy
2 garlic cloves, minced
1 piece fresh ginger, minced
1 medium onion
any handy vegetables, chopped
1 teaspoon curry powder or paste
vegetable oil

Sauté the garlic, ginger, onion, and curry powder or paste in a little oil. When the onion is wilted, add the vegetables and mix thoroughly. Add the beef chunks and gravy. Simmer a half hour. Serve with Uncle Ben's rice. Note: A nearly instant curry can be made by heating garlic, curry powder, and ginger in oil and simply adding canned beef.

QUICK CHUTNEY

1 can whole cranberry sauce
fresh ginger
1 garlic clove

Mince the garlic and ginger very fine. Mix into the cranberry sauce and allow the flavors to get acquainted for a couple of hours.

Here's another main dish using canned beef chunks. It can be dressed up or down depending on the cook's imagination.

SAILOR'S SHEPHERD PIE

canned beef chunks in gravy
instant mashed potatoes
dry milk
herbs
salt and pepper
butter

Put the beef in a baking dish, adding whatever herbs you wish. Add the mashed potatoes and butter. Bake in the galley oven 20 minutes or so, until the crust is golden brown.

For the first night out, you might want to serve fillets made of beef tenderloin. These need only be garnished with canned baby potatoes browned in butter and parsley and a fresh green salad.

FIRST-NIGHT FILLETS

fillets of beef
butter
Burgundy
salt and pepper
sliced French bread

Brown the fillets in a little butter, leaving the meat rare in the center. Set aside a moment and brown slices of bread in butter in another pan. Take the pan you've cooked the fillets in, turn up the heat, and add some Burgundy. Boil quickly to reduce the sauce. Place each fillet on a crouton and pour sauce over them. Enjoy the rest of the Burgundy with the meal.

DESSERTS UNDER SAIL

Here's a smattering of desserts that help keep spirits up in the doldrums or after a long day of close-hauled sailing. Bananas may be sliced and fried in butter along with a good sprinkle of brown sugar. If you wish, dribble a little rum on them at the end and flame them. According to Emily, no other liquor tastes as good as rum does on the water. For centuries the British Navy gave a rum ration to its seamen for good reason!

For long voyages, when ready access to civilization is not available, a little dessert is a comfort. The Hunters used boxed pudding mixes with great success. Emily mixed them with undiluted evaporated milk. The result is a rich dessert.

Try mixing vanilla pudding mix with the milk and adding a bit of rum and grated orange peel. Serve warm.

Chocolate pudding mix marries well with canned mandarin orange slices and a spot of Grand Marnier.

For variation, pour a can of raspberries that have been jostling around aboard ship over warm vanilla pudding. The combination of sweet and tart is irresistible.

Soak dried apricots in a little water for several hours and toss them with walnut or pecan halves. Again, add a drop of rum for a late-evening snack.

We have some friends at Rowley's Bay who live at the mouth of the Mink River. Each time I visit I feel I've left the peninsula proper. The feeling is of lake country, but somewhere else. Cedar woods dominate the landscape, and the shoreline is marshy, with bulrushes and water lilies in profusion. It is *Wind in the Willows* transported, and I expect to see Toad, Mole, and Rat come along in a little boat at any moment.

When my daughter Julie and her friend Justine take a canoe up river, they go alone through the rushes to a secret hideaway. Adults are not invited. Sometimes they take an old-fashioned English tea in a small wicker hamper.

Aynsley's English Tea in a Hamper
cress sandwiches
scones
Door County cherry preserve
hard-boiled eggs
peppermint tea in a flask

CRESS SANDWICHES

garden cress or watercress, chopped
butter
thin-sliced bread with the crusts cut off

Any child can put these together. Make lots—they disappear in a moment. The Wagon Wheel Bakery at Rowley's Bay makes fine bread.

ROWLEY'S BAY SCONES

2 cups flour
3 teaspoons baking powder
2 tablespoons sugar
6 tablespoons shortening
½ teaspoon salt
2½ cups buttermilk

Sift the dry ingredients. Cut in the shortening until the mixture is crumbly. Add the buttermilk, mixing only enough to moisten the flour. Too much mixing makes for tough scones. Turn the mixture onto a lightly floured board and pat into a round about 1 inch thick. Cut into 12 pie-shaped pieces. Place on a greased cookie sheet and bake in a 400-degree oven 18 to 20 minutes.

When I think of a lighthouse, I recall Virginia Woolf's wonderful novel *To the Lighthouse*, and I am one with the Ramseys in waiting for a fair day to get there. What is it in us all that finds these places of great importance to visit, explore, sketch, and photograph?

Door County has more than its share of lighthouses if one were to judge by land mass. The one in Peninsula State Park is a jewel, outfitted with the everyday necessities of a hundred years ago. In the summer, it is open to visitors, many of whom, after examining the furnishings, have wished to move in.

The little beauty at the tip of Rock Island is my own private idea of the ultimate getaway, even though I haven't a clue as to its interior, boarded up as it is.

On excursions to a lighthouse, I take a picnic. Here's one that should travel nicely, whether you go by land or by sea.

Lighthouse Picnic
1 small roasted chicken
cucumber sandwiches
cherry tomatoes and mushrooms
yogurt dip for vegetables
individual cherry tarts
wine of your choice

ROASTED CHICKEN WITH MUSTARD

1 chicken
1 pot Dijon-style mustard
2 cloves garlic, chopped
1 onion, peeled
fresh ground pepper

Coat the chicken with mustard inside and out. I find this easiest to do with my fingers. Stick the onion and the garlic into the chicken. Dust with pepper if you wish. Put in a heavy roasting pot with a bit of oil. Cover and roast at 375 degrees for an hour. Remove the lid. Turn the oven up to 450 degrees and brown the skin. Five minutes should do it. Serve hot or cold.

CUCUMBER SANDWICHES

1 cucumber
several slices bread
butter

These are very plain sandwiches, and they are delectable. The bread should be sliced very thin. So should the cucumber. Butter the bread covering the entire surface, and arrange slices of cucumbers to cover. Slice off the crusts and cut in dainty shapes if you wish. Chill.

When I was young, in Wisconsin, hunting went on "up north." No matter where you lived, hunting went on north of that. The mythic getaway to the Elysian Fields.

So we have "up north" in the Horicon Marsh, or on a Lake Winnebago slough, or near Tipler, or in Door County.

In those days women weren't invited. The husband brought home the provender along with his dirty laundry, and the wife washed and cooked. The children picked the burrs or porky quills out of the dog. The hunter cleaned the game if he hadn't already done that in camp. The family feasted. And while they ate they listened to hunting stories.

Tall tales? Absolutely not. Each story had the ring of ironclad truth. And if Chester or Sam had been at the table, he'd be willing to swear on the family Bible. Every aspect of the trip was described in superlatives: the card games, the jokes, the coffee and camp food, not to mention the number of birds bagged by each hunter.

There are hunting shacks all over Wisconsin, going back to the days when you could take fifty coots and perhaps eighty bluebills in a day. Hunting has always been a sport of kings, but the industrialist scions such as Ringling and Pullman went off to sleep on straw mattresses just like any millworker camping up the way. Baths were unheard of; no shack had a shaving mirror, nor did the stalwart hunters pack a razor.

Hunters I've known talk about a gigantic hunting camp bed, an oblong structure of ten-inch logs, seven feet deep and perhaps fourteen or fifteen feet long. Each year a rick of fresh straw was dumped in after the previous year's had been retired. This Bunyanesque bed could sleep ten to fifteen hunters at one time. One wonders how many boilermakers a hunter would have to drink to assure a good night's sleep wedged in with eight or nine of his boon companions.

Whether any peninsula hunting shack has a bed to equal it, I don't know. Still, the county has its share of shacks and duck blinds, most of them inaccessible to an uninvited guest. They're located where the waterfowl hunting is at its best,

36 WATER AND SHORE

in the marshy shoreline areas. We could begin looking around Sturgeon Bay, both lake and bayside, then move north to North Bay on Lake Michigan and along to the tip of the landmass. Both the Mink River and Mud Lake are legendary for bagging fowl.

Partridge can be taken throughout the county and especially at the edge of cedar swamps adjoining the lakeshore. I've surprised them often in the upper Door. These days pheasants are scarce, but not so deer, who, if you can bear to shoot them, range the entire county as well as Washington Island and even Chambers.

Wild game wants racier accompaniments than white potatoes and rice. Wild rice, red cabbage, lingonberries, cranberries, juniper berries, chanterelle mushrooms, and yams bring out and enhance the flavor.

Rumor has had it, as long as I've been around these parts, that wild rice can be gathered on the Mink River. I've not found any yet. Elsewhere in Wisconsin and in Minnesota the American Indian has recornered both the gathering places and the market. The price per pound is always dear and, I believe, well worth paying.

Following is a slew of recipes for cooking wild game.

MUD LAKE MALLARDS

2 mallard ducks
¼ cup butter
2 tablespoons olive oil
juice and rind of 2 limes
4 ounces brandy
6 to 8 juniper berries
1 cup light broth
salt and pepper

Preheat the oven to 300 degrees. Rinse the birds in salted cold water. Wipe them dry. Wipe the birds liberally with lime juice and 2 ounces of brandy. Pour some of the liquid into the cavity of each bird. Season with salt and pepper and brown lightly in the butter and olive oil. Place the birds in the roaster. Pour 2 ounces of heated brandy over the birds, and light. Allow the flames to burn out. Arrange the strips of lime rind and juniper berries inside and around the birds. Add a bit of broth. Cover the roaster and bake for 1½ hours, basting occasionally. Remove the cover and continue to roast until the birds are browned and done.

COOT STEW FROM MUD LAKE

2 mud hens (coots)
6 small onions, chopped
8 carrots, chopped
6 tomatoes, peeled and
  coarsely chopped
4 tablespoons chopped
  parsley
2 bay leaves
¼ teaspoon marjoram
3 tablespoons vinegar
6 juniper berries
salt and pepper
flour

Skin the birds, removing the legs, breasts, and thighs. Discard the remaining pieces. Place all the other ingredients in a large, heavy cocotte and bring to a simmer. Salt and pepper the fowl and dust with flour. Brown in a bit of butter or oil and add to the vegetables. Cover and simmer slowly for 2 hours. Serves 2 generously or 4 in a pinch.

PARTRIDGE IN A POT

2 partridges
2 cups chicken broth
¼ cup currant jelly
butter
flour
salt and pepper

Shake the birds in flour seasoned with salt and pepper. Brown them in butter. Arrange the birds breast up in a roasting pan and add a half cup stock. Bring to a boil and reduce the heat immediately to simmer. Cover and cook for 1 hour. Add stock as needed and baste frequently. When the birds are tender, remove them to a heated platter. Add the currant jelly to the pan juices. Boil and reduce by ¼. Serve the sauce separately.

WILD GOOSE AND RED CABBAGE

1 goose
1 medium-sized head red cabbage, sliced
½ cup vinegar
2 tablespoons sugar
1 teaspoon pickling spices
salt and pepper
flour
butter and oil
1 cup light stock

Cut the goose into serving pieces. Split the breast in two. Season with salt and pepper and dredge in flour. Brown in a combination of oil and butter. Add half the stock, cover, and simmer for about an hour. Remove the goose while you add the cabbage. Sprinkle the cabbage with the pickling spices and add the vinegar, stock, and sugar. Put the goose back into the pot, cover, and continue to cook over a low flame until the ingredients are tender, at least one hour. Remove the cabbage and goose to a heated platter and reduce the pan juices to gravy consistency. Degrease the juices if necessary. Pour the gravy over the goose and serve.

VENISON POT ROAST

haunch or loin of venison
salt pork for larding
3 medium onions
4 carrots
2 to 3 turnips
4 stalks celery
parsley, chopped
pinch rosemary
pinch thyme
1 bay leaf
several strips lemon peel
salt and pepper
red wine
sour cream
olive oil

Trim the venison. Lard it with salt pork. (See any basic cookbook for larding directions.) Chop all the vegetables and sauté them in oil in a heavy pot. When the vegetables are limp but not brown, add a cup of red wine and a cup of water or stock. Cover and simmer a half hour. Rub the venison with herbs, salt and pepper it, and put it in the pot with the lemon peel laid over and under it. Cover and simmer for approximately 2 hours or until the venison is tender. Remove the meat and vegetables to a heated platter. Strain the sauce and add at least a half cup of sour cream. Cook slowly for several minutes without bringing the sauce to a boil. Serve the sauce with the venison. Serves 6.

WOODCOCK STUFFED WITH LINGONBERRIES

1 scallion, chopped fine
1 stalk celery, chopped fine
1 cup dry vermouth
2 pinches chervil
1 pinch tarragon
¾ cup breadcrumbs
½ cup preserved lingonberries
1 ounce brandy
1/8 pound melted butter
1 cup heavy cream
salt and pepper
2 woodcocks

Combine the wine, celery, scallion, and herbs in a small saucepan and simmer for 10 minutes. Strain the liquid and reserve it. Combine the breadcrumbs (which you've browned in butter), lingonberries, and strained vegetables in a bowl. Add the brandy and enough melted butter to make a moist stuffing. Next, rub the birds inside and out with salt and pepper. Stuff the birds and truss them. Coat the birds with melted butter, place in small roasting pan, and roast them for 5 minutes at 400 degrees. Then reduce the heat to 300 degrees and roast for at least 30 minutes, basting often with the reserved liquid and the rest of the melted butter. When the birds are tender, transfer them to a heated platter. Add 1 cup of heavy cream to the pan juices and make a gravy. Pour this sauce over the birds and serve immediately.

Pheasants are scarcer than hens' teeth in Door County. They do not winter over well, and consequently, the state has stopped "planting" them. If you should find a survivor during the season and bring it home in your game bag, here's a plain but elegant way to cook it.

WINE-BAKED PHEASANT

1 pheasant cut in serving pieces
½ cup or more red wine
½ teaspoon rosemary
4 or 5 juniper berries
⅛ pound butter, melted
1 clove garlic, chopped fine
salt and pepper
flour

Season the pheasant pieces with salt and pepper, shake in flour, and brown on all sides in the melted butter, which has been brought nearly to the smoking point. Add the rosemary, juniper berries, garlic, and wine. Cover and bake at 325 degrees for 2 hours or until the birds are tender. Serve with wild rice, lingonberries, and a green salad. Serves 4.

Once I received a magic Christmas present from a friend: an antique beaded bag stuffed full of Wisconsin wild rice. I opened the bag and the rice spilled out on the white countertop. Because it was Christmas Day, I pushed each precious kernal into a sieve, rinsed the rice several times, and put it on to cook, accompanied by the innards of the turkey.

Cooking wild rice is true child's play and an easy way for a beginning cook to have a stunning success at a dinner party. Let's say you have the birds and the hunter to cook them. All you need do is buy the best dinner rolls available, make a large salad, and bring out the bowl of wild rice and mushrooms as a clincher to the meal.

WILD RICE FOR BEGINNERS

1 cup wild rice
3 cups broth or water
1 tablespoon butter
1 teaspoon salt (if using water)
1 cup frozen green peas
1 cup sautéed mushrooms

Rinse the rice in a fine sieve several times. Put the rice, water, salt, and butter in a heavy saucepan with a close-fitting lid. Bring to a boil and stir. Turn to simmer and cook until each grain is tender and separate. Cooking time varies, as each harvest differs. From 1 to 1 ½ hours is average. Do not worry about the rice becoming sticky. Unlike domestic rice, this wild grain does not contain a great amount of gluten. Before serving, stir in the sautéed mushrooms and a cup of uncooked frozen peas. Cook a few minutes longer. Serves 6 to 8.

Red cabbage enhances wild game of any description. Here's a Scandinavian version.

RED CABBAGE AND APPLES

1 large red cabbage, shredded
3 tablespoons butter
2 tablespoons molasses
3 apples, peeled and sliced
1 onion, grated fine
juice 1 lemon
½ cup dry red wine
good pinch salt

Melt the butter in a large, heavy pot. Add the cabbage, apples, and molasses. Brown over moderate heat, stirring constantly. Add the remaining ingredients. Cover and simmer several hours, stirring occasionally and adding a bit of stock if the mixture seems to be drying out. This dish tastes best the second day, so make in advance to serve with wild game. Serves 6.

RED CABBAGE SALAD

1 red cabbage
1 large apple
several stalks celery
1 cup whipping cream
juice 1 small lemon
½ teaspoon salt
1 tablespoon sugar

Take off the outer leaves and grate or chop the cabbage very fine. Cut the apple in small pieces and chop the celery fine. Whip the cream. Mix the vegetables with the lemon juice, salt, and sugar. Fold in the cream.

Lingonberries in the wild are surely as scarce as bears in Door County. After years of trying to track down rumored lingonberries growing near the Toft property on the eastern side of the peninsula, I've given up. I buy conserve at groceries and shops up here and serve it with any wild game that comes my way.

Juniper berries may be used to advantage with game. They are strong in flavor, and a few go a long way. Sprinkle them in the cavities of birds to be roasted; include them in dressings and marinades.

Juniper berries are sold in specialty shops at trendy prices. You needn't be too clever to forage your own. Look for juniper shrubs or trees in the more barren parts of the county. The berries are blue-black, with a pale white bloom on the berry itself. Dry them on a sunny day and store them in glass jars. Or, if you are a moonshiner, you'll want to use them in flavoring your best gin.

Of all the wild animals and birds I've sighted over the years feeding at water's edge, the one I'd most like to see is the fabled bear. He's been into the honey on Blackberry Road, eaten all the laying hens on a farm near Sister Bay, helped himself to cherries at a Valmy Orchard, and recently been seen crossing a road near Fish Creek at noon by a young friend of mine who has all his wits about him.

For years I thought this bear had winged feet to cover so much ground. Now I hear there are twenty to forty black bears in the county. How did they get here? They came on ice floes, one source told me, just came along from the Upper Peninsula of Michigan like the timber wolves do.

But legend dies hard. I expect some moonlit night to look out and see the famous traveling bear eating apples off our old tree. Pawing them down, one by one, standing tall on his hind legs.

I couldn't shoot him, no more than I could shoot the little fox that strolls through our garden at dusk. No recipe for bear stew here.

Living up here at the tip of the peninsula with only a canoe to paddle through Death's Door and beyond, we sometimes take the ferry to Washington Island, dragging our bikes along.

The island has its lure for mainlanders, and the ferry ride is a must in Door County. The ferries, constructed with wide, flat bottoms to fight winter ice floes and wild water, ply all day in and out of the harbor, loaded with people eager to have a look and, for the bulk of them, a quick return.

The ferry ride lasts thirty-five minutes in good weather and is just long enough to whet an appetite without compelling us to eat all our backpacked stores aboard ship. We find Washington Island a lovely place for cycling—explorable in a day, with good roads on the flats.

Perhaps the most crowded and exciting time to be on the island in summer is during the Scandinavian Festival in early August, which combines folk dancing and smorgasbord eating. I prefer a weekday visit, when the roads are uncrowded. We head straight for Sand Dunes Beach for a quick swim, enjoy a leisurely ride to Jackson Harbor at the top of the island, ride west to Washington Harbor, and finally head up to the tip (Boyer's Bluff, famous to nearly every sport fisherman in these parts), where we visit a small, perfect lake, aptly named Little Lake, and the Jacobsen Museum close by.

At the museum, we examine and exclaim over the collection of Indian artifacts, some of them from the Copper Age, and the local fossils, which we have replicas of at home. We admire the intricate jigsaw work, which one onlooker nicely termed gramp art.

By this time, we're starved for food and a look at Little Lake. It is special, being a lake within a lake, and so beautiful that had Thoreau found it, he would have claimed it another Walden Pond. A frog is generally sitting on a pad among the lilies, and sometimes a heron out on a half-sunken log. A wide-angle lens might take in all the beauty, but since we have none, we stare and eat instead.

These biking picnics are usually bare bones: apples, Wisconsin cheddar and summer sausage, children's crackers, and a thermos of lemonade or tea to pass around.

Children's crackers may be made easily by children, but adults usually manage to finish them off.

CRACKERS

2 cups cornmeal
2½ cups whole wheat flour
1 tablespoon salt
¾ cup sunflower oil
½ cup sesame or poppy seeds

Mix all the ingredients until crumbly. Add enough water to make a sticky dough, approximately 1¼ cups. Press all around in a cookie sheet, roll with a glass, and score. Bake in a 350-degree oven for about 40 minutes, until golden brown. For a Scandinavian flavor, use equal parts of cornmeal, whole wheat, and rye flour and throw in some caraway seeds.

On another occasion, we might pull out all the stops and bring a fancy Scandinavian picnic: anchovy-stuffed eggs, tongue salad, limpa, strawberries, and white seedless grapes. Plastic containers and small paper plates and cups make this meal portable by bike. Two splits of Riesling, one for each backpack, accompany the feast. We always leave a corkscrew in a backpack, having learned the hard way we don't do well without it.

ANCHOVY-STUFFED EGGS

4 hard-boiled eggs
5 tablespoons butter
10 anchovy fillets
white pepper
chopped parsley
chopped chives

Peel and split the boiled eggs. Remove the yolks. Pass the yolks, butter, and anchovy fillets through a sieve. Season to taste. Fill the egg whites. Fit together. Wrap with waxed paper, chill, and put in a plastic container for carrying.

Even if your family is not vegetarian, tongue may be a chancy matter. My family will eat it, providing they do not have to see it, at any stage of the game, until it is sliced and *in* something—like a salad or a sandwich.

BOILING A WHOLE TONGUE

4- to 5-pound tongue
2 celery stalks, sliced
2 carrots, sliced
1 onion stuck with 3 cloves
2 bay leaves
good pinch salt
6 peppercorns
2 cloves garlic

Take a large kettle, fill with cold water, and add all the ingredients. Bring to a fast boil and skim off the foam. Reduce to a simmer and cook the tongue 3 hours or until easily pierced with a knife. Cool the tongue in its own liquid. Skin it and slice very thin with a sharp knife. Serve with a horseradish mayonnaise or make the following salad.

TONGUE SALAD

2 cups julienne tongue slices
1 cup diced celery
1 diced apple sprinkled with lemon juice
3 tablespoons diced gherkins
6 or 7 sliced stuffed olives
1 head best lettuce
handful chopped parsley
1 cup mustard French dressing

For a picnic, put all the ingredients except the dressing into a plastic container. Chill until ready to leave the house. Put the salad dressing into a large plastic vitamin bottle and wrap that in a plastic bag. Mustard French dressing is made by combining a vinegar and oil dressing with a heaped spoonful of Dijon mustard. Mix everything together just before eating. 6 generous servings.

On the ferry ride home we speculate on the fate of the *Griffin*, the sailing ship that left Detroit Harbor in September 1679 loaded with fur pelts and simply disappeared. And always, in rough or calm water, when we enter Death's Door we think of the dozens of ships whose bones lie on the lake bottom below us.

After a day of outdoor exercise, there's nothing I like more than to come home to a meal already prepared. Unless the evening is very warm, a bowl of soup suits perfectly.

SCANDINAVIAN YELLOW PEA SOUP

2 cups dried yellow peas
2 quarts water
1 pound pork steak or salted side pork
2 teaspoons salt
1 onion sliced in two
white pepper
good pinch ginger

Soak the peas overnight. Bring the peas and the water to a boil in a large, heavy kettle. Cook vigorously until the shells come off. As they float to the surface, skim them off and discard. Add the pork and other ingredients and simmer slowly for several hours. Serve the pork on the side with a sharp mustard.

Pickled beets are a good accompaniment. They may be made with fresh or canned beets.

PICKLED BEETS

2 dozen small beets

Dressing:
1 cup white vinegar
4 tablespoons water
4 tablespoons sugar
2 cloves

Cook the beets whole in boiling, salted water about 40 minutes, until tender. Drain and peel away the skin. Cut in thin slices. Place in a shallow dish and pour dressing over them. Let them sit most of the day in the dressing. Store in the refrigerator.

WOODS·AND·BYWAYS

It is late spring in the county. The trillium are fading to a soft dusty pink, and the cherry blossoms are just coming on. I'm sitting in the screened sleeping porch of our old house. Mixed with the windy smell of big water blowing through the woods is another, tender and sweet, overlaid with an elusive scent of mushrooms. It's the smell of growing things, and in this clean country air it is almost piercing in its signal of spring.

Earlier this morning the lure was too strong, and I gave up the typewriter to go out wandering on foot, first tucking several paper bags and a knife into my pack. Whatever greens I might forage for supper salad were secondary. I had a case of mushroom fever. Morel fever to be exact.

I hold Euell Gibbons in some part responsible. With his book *Stalking the Wild Asparagus*, he put wild edibles back on the map. The spate of books which followed were a part of the back-to-the-land revolution in American culture that has caused us to build our own houses from scratch, to garden and preserve with ferocity, to make wood splitting a sport that vies with pro football, and to set thousands of foragers out into the remnants of our wilderness to search for provender.

Still, this county has room for all of us. I've never run into another mushroom hunter in the hours I've spent at the sport.

Caution in red letters is the word for mushroom hunting, a sport more potentially dangerous than hang gliding. The first rule is the most important: NEVER EAT A WILD MUSHROOM UNLESS YOU ARE ABSOLUTELY CERTAIN IT IS NOT POISONOUS.

A mistake can mean your life. Some of the most beautiful looking mushrooms will whisk you off the planet. But not in a hurry. Delayed action of the poison makes first aid useless and causes a slow and excruciating death. The *Amanita* destroying angel is a case in point.

The angel stands, an elegant white sentinel in the woods, so beautiful that one is drawn to examine it. Its purity suggests delicate servings with drawn butter on china plates. But beware, and do not pick. Learn all *Amanita* by sight; take none of them home, not even for observation.

Despite these black words of warning, there are seven or eight easily recognizable mushrooms that you may eat with a calm head and stomach, once you learn them. The chanterelle, the giant puffball, the meadow mushroom, the morel, the shaggy mane, the oyster, and the giant boletus are all choice and delicious. I've found all of them except for the giant boletus right here in the county.

Learn mushrooms from an expert. The walks sponsored by the Ridges Sanctuary and given by Charlotte Luckes are a good way to begin. Courses are being offered all across the country. Avail yourself of the chance to learn firsthand in the field.

Buy several field guides and read them with care. *The Mushroom Hunter's Field Guide* by Alexander H. Smith (University of Michigan Press) is still the bible for the Midwest, for much of Smith's fieldwork was done in Michigan. The photos are clear, generally to scale, and frequently in color.

Door County is a feast of wild, edible fungi, providing weather conditions are right. My advice is to choose several "easy" mushrooms and enjoy the search.

I'd take a morel to any of them, wild or cultivated. So will many other foragers, and consequently, no one is giving away any secret hunting grounds. Morels are commonly called sponge mushrooms to many Midwest farm families, and stories abound of picking washtubs full once the season is on. The shape of the morel is conical, with small indentations over the outside surface of the cap. Morels may be so perfectly camouflaged in their environment that a forager may walk right over them.

The morel spore has been patented, but no commercial mushroom cultivator has been able to produce a single mushroom. Nature keeps her secrets well. Consequently, the price of a small jar of imported morels may run upward of twenty dollars in a speciality food shop.

I'd rather pick my own right here in the county.

MORELS IN BUTTER

3 handfuls morels
1 large lump butter
1 teaspoon fresh lemon juice (optional)

Split the morels in two lengthwise and run them under cold water. Pat them dry with a clean towel. Heat the butter and frizzle the morels, tossing them in the pan to cover all surfaces. Serve them immediately, as they are, on warm plates or sprinkle with lemon juice at the last moment. Serves 4.

MORELS IN SOUR HALF-AND-HALF

4 cups morels
1 large lump butter
1 cup sour half-and-half
paprika
toast points or rice

Split and clean the morels. Sauté them in butter. Add Wisconsin sour half-and-half, taking care not to let it come to a boil. Serve on toast points or rice. Sprinkle each serving with paprika. Serves 4 to 6.

For stuffed mushroom fans, here is the ultimate: a lovely honeymoon supper or a supreme snack with champagne.

STUFFED MORELS

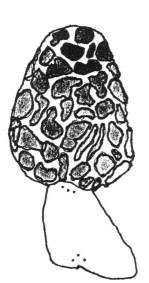

2 cups morels
½ pound chicken livers
butter
flour
salt and pepper to taste
2 teaspoons sherry
parsley, chopped fine

Parboil the morels by dropping them into boiling water for a few minutes. Drain. Remove the stems and chop fine. Cook the chicken livers in butter, adding sherry for the last 2 or 3 minutes of sautéing time. Remove the livers from the heat and chop. Combine the livers, the morel stems, and a handful of chopped parsley. Add the cooking juices from the livers. Split the morels and stuff them with the mixture. Lay on a buttered baking pan. Bake in a 350-degree oven for about 15 minutes, basting occasionally with melted butter. Serve immediately. Serves 2 to 6.

Here is a refined French version of an old American standard. Serve this to children only if you wish to fool them into developing gourmet appetites.

MORELS AND MACARONI A LA CRÈME

1 pound macaroni
6 tablespoons butter
1 pound Swiss cheese, grated
4 egg yolks, gently beaten
2 cups cream
1 cup morels, chopped fine
pinch nutmeg
salt and pepper

Boil the macaroni and drain. Melt the butter in a large, heavy-bottomed pan. Frizzle the morels for a minute. Add the macaroni, the egg yolks mixed with the cream, and the cheese. Mix the cheese in gradually as you stir and lift over a low heat. When all the ingredients have reached a creamy consistency (this will be in a matter of minutes), stir in the nutmeg and salt and pepper to taste. Heap this delicious mess on a large, deep platter and garnish with tomato slices. Serves 8 to 12, depending on appetites. This rich dish will benefit by being served with a tart green salad.

The other day, at a flea market south of here, I saw a huge cluster of oyster mushrooms, dried and varnished. I can't imagine what one would do with them—perhaps a gift for a friend one wishes to forget or a midnight planting in a neighbor's garden where the bulbs failed to show. I'd much rather see them growing on a stump or a fallen log, ready to be pulled off and cooked. Oyster mushrooms are generally pale cream with a faintly lavender cast, bearing a very slight resemblance to oysters on the half shell. They fruit in abundance on old stumps or fallen and decaying logs. Spring and fall are the times to search.

The last clump I took home weighed seven pounds. I rang up friends and said, "Come for supper."

SERENDIPITY OYSTER FRY

4 large fistfuls oyster mushrooms
2 or 3 beaten eggs
3 tablespoons water
flour
parsley clusters
peanut oil
butter

Remove the tough stems and soak the mushrooms in lightly salted water. Some little guys may come crawling out. Don't be alarmed. This does not mean the mushrooms are spoiled. Pull off sections of the mushrooms and dip them in a mix of beaten egg and water. Dredge them in flour; dip again in the egg mix and again in flour. Meanwhile heat a 4-to-1 mixture of peanut oil and butter in a deep, heavy frying pan. Fry the mushrooms quickly, turning them from one side to the other. Remove them to absorbent paper and then to a hot platter. Turn up the heat under the skillet until the oil is nearly smoking. Drop in the parsley fronds and quick-fry them. Remove, drain, and arrange around the mushrooms. Serve right away. Serves 8.

I fed this dish to a crowd. It was my basic spur-of-the-moment feast, which includes a main dish, a loaf of Cuban bread, and a large green salad.

Cuban bread is a pushover. It can be put together in a hurry after work or a day at the beach and served hot for supper.

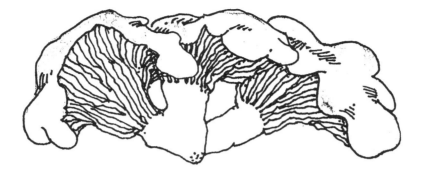

CUBAN BREAD IN GILLS ROCK

1 envelope yeast
2 cups water, warm
2 teaspoons salt
1 teaspoon sugar
1 tablespoon olive oil
5 to 6 cups flour
cornmeal

Put the warm water, yeast, sugar, oil, and salt in your favorite bread-making bowl. Mix and allow to sit and get acquainted for a few minutes. Begin mixing in the flour, cup by cup. When the dough is sticky but workable, dust your hands liberally with flour and knead the dough for several minutes. Butter the top of the dough and put it into the oven to rise. I hurry this process by setting the oven at 400 degrees for a matter of seconds and then turning it off. When the dough has nearly doubled in volume, punch it down, shape it into a round flat loaf, and put it on a cookie sheet that has been dusted with cornmeal. Sprinkle cornmeal on the top of the dough and slash it crosswise with a sharp knife. Put on the middle rack of the oven and turn the oven on to 375 degrees. The bread should be baked in 50 to 55 minutes. Remove and serve hot.

I spent years searching for chanterelles in the Colorado Rockies, only to find my first one in a beech, maple, and pine woods near Ellison Bay. Never having seen one in the flesh (except under cream sauce in a French restaurant), I declined to eat my prize. I handed it over to an expert for verification and for assurance it wasn't a jack-o'-lantern (*Clitocybe illudens*), which bears some resemblance and is poisonous.

To my delight, the chanterelle was the real thing, and we've been eating them ever since. This mushroom fruits in Door County following a rainy season in late July and early August. It is fluted in shape, with long, wavy gills. The color is a strong yellow-orange, and it smells like apricot

The flesh is firm and dense; consequently, chanterelles require longer cooking than most mushrooms, and they keep well. They also dry and freeze beautifully. Kings, queens, and other elegant eaters have prized these mushrooms for centuries.

DRYING CHANTERELLES

I've tried to dry chanterelles in the oven with no success—I've not been able to get the heat low enough. I'd advise using the old-fashioned method of drying them on screens. Slice the mushrooms in two if they are large, lay them on clean screens, and keep them in a warm, balmy place for 24 hours. Jiggle the screens several times during the drying period to make sure all surfaces are exposed to air and light. Good luck with our Door County humidity!

FREEZING CHANTERELLES

Make a solution of 1 teaspoon lemon juice to 1 pint water. Clean and slice the chanterelles into thick, uniform pieces. Soak the mushrooms in the solution for 5 minutes. Drain, pat dry with clean towels, and freeze.

Should you want to run off to the beach on a hot day in late July and need a presto brunch to take along, make an individual omelet wrapped in flour tortilla or pita (Arab pocket bread). Add to your provender a bag full of fresh fruit and a thermos of coffee or tea.

CHANTERELLE PICNIC OMELET

chanterelles, sliced
several thin slices ham
flour tortilla or pita
butter
parsley, chopped
chives, chopped
salt and pepper to taste

Sauté the sliced chanterelles in butter until done. Toss the ham slices with them for the last few minutes. Remove and keep warm. Make an omelet using one large egg. At the last minute, slip in the mushrooms and ham, and sprinkle with salt, pepper, chives, and parsley. Put the omelet aside for a moment while you heat the flour tortilla. Slip in the omelet, roll it up, and wrap in a piece of foil. Tuck into a section of last Sunday's newspaper for more insulation, and you're set for the beach.

ABOUT FLOUR TORTILLAS

Many midwesterners complain they don't enjoy flour tortillas. I suspect this is because they don't know how to finish the cooking process. Flour tortillas have much in common with brown-and-serve rolls. They are half done when you buy them. The trick is to make them ready for eating without scorching or making them brittle. Southwesterners use either the top of a wood stove, a gas burner, or a greased griddle. The griddle is the easiest method. Heat a greased griddle nearly to the smoking point. Drop the tortilla on the griddle. Press down all over the surface with a spatula. Turn once and do the same on the other side. Do *not* turn again, as this is what makes the tortilla stiff and brittle. A perfectly cooked tortilla is hot, limp, and not greasy. (The same method should be used for corn tortillas. Only gringos eat their tacos in crisp cooked tortillas.)

Flour tortillas are traditionally served in southwestern restaurants instead of bread. They are presented at the table wrapped in napkins with a small dish of butter on the side.

A last word on chanterelles. They will be happy in any recipe employing mushrooms, such as stews, meat loaves, and soups. I don't waste the following soup on any guest or family member who feels squeamish about wild mushrooms.

CREAM OF CHANTERELLE SOUP SUPREME

3 to 4 cups chanterelles, sliced fine
6 tablespoons butter
1 tablespoon lemon juice
1 handful chopped parsley
good pinch chervil
several scallions, finely chopped
3 tablespoons flour
5 to 6 cups fresh chicken broth
good pinch thyme
salt and pepper
½ cup heavy cream
1 tablespoon sherry

Heat the butter in a large, heavy pot. Sauté the mushrooms, herbs, and scallions until they are limp and nearly cooked. Work in the flour completely. Stir and cook approximately 1 minute. Add the hot chicken broth gradually, taking care not to make lumps of the flour. Add the lemon juice. Cook 45 minutes over low heat. Add the cream slowly., taking care not to curdle it. Add the sherry and simmer a few more minutes. Salt and pepper to taste. Serve in big soup plates with dark bread and sweet butter. Serves 8.

The pleasure of a long solitary walk through the countryside is not to be underestimated. Given most Door County households during the summer—filled with children, family, and out-of-state guests—the cook in particular may need to escape. Rewards may be various: a bird never spotted before, a jack-in the-pulpit in a forest glen, an old whiskey flask sprouting from a stump, or a mess of greens for supper.

Some of us grew up with grandmothers or uncles who could forage their way across country. Others went to camp and learned a few edible plants. Most of us could benefit from a nature walk at the Ridges.

I have a friend who picked a bouquet of dried weeds and berries in November. She swelled up for a week. It took three doctors to determine she had a case of poison ivy out of season.

Among the other poisonous plants a forager ought to recognize are nightshade, hemlock, jimsonweed, fool's parsley, and baneberry. All of them have slightly sinister names.

Still, there are any number of edible plants a child could identify. The common dandelion ranks first among them. Dandelion greens ought to be picked when they are in their tender youth, otherwise they will be bitter. Blossoms for wine, however, are picked in maturity.

DANDELION WINE

1 gallon dandelion flowers
1 gallon boiling water
3 oranges, sliced fine
3 lemons, sliced fine
3 pounds sugar
1 ounce yeast

Set the children to work. My father used to pay me a penny a dozen for every bunch I could dig up by the roots. What any child would rather do is pick the flowers. Let them. But insist that no bitter stems get into the pail with the blossoms. Press the blossoms into a 2-gallon crock. Pour the boiling water over them and leave the crock for 3 days, covered with cheesecloth. Then strain the liquid through the cheesecloth and squeeze out all the juice. Put the dandelion juice, with the rinds and pulp of the fruit, into the crock. Stir in the sugar. Add the yeast. Stir again and cover. Put aside for 3 weeks while the wine ferments. Strain and funnel into sterilized bottles. Cork the wine.

WILTED DANDELION SALAD

4 large handfuls dandelion greens
6 slices bacon
3 tablespoons vinegar
1 tablespoon sugar
salt and pepper to taste

Put the cleaned greens into a salad bowl. Cook the bacon until crisp, but take care not to burn the fat. Remove the bacon and crumble over the greens. Mix the grease, vinegar, sugar, and salt and pepper quickly, and pour over the greens, tossing all the while. Eat right away. 6 small servings.

GREENS AND EGGS

4 eggs
water
1 cup dandelion greens, shredded
bacon grease
salt and pepper to taste

Beat the eggs lightly and mix in a couple teaspoons of water. Add the greens. Heat the grease in a skillet. Scramble the eggs. Serve with hot cornmeal muffins.

I foraged my last fiddleheads from a Maine flea market at one dollar a pound. In Boston gourmet shops, they run over three dollars. In Door County, I could have them for free.

Fiddleheads are my absolute favorite of the spring greens. They are the tightly curled fronds of the ostrich fern, caught before opening. Look for them in dense, rich woods or by streams and marshy places. Get rid of the scaley brown coverings by rubbing them lightly between your fingers before cooking. The taste can only be described by saying they are sweeter than asparagus.

STEAMED FIDDLEHEADS

Nothing could be simpler. Clean the fiddleheads. Steam them in your vegetable cooker and toss them with melted butter. Salt, pepper, and enjoy!

FIDDLEHEAD SOUP

2 cups fiddleheads, cleaned
4 cups chicken broth
salt and pepper
1 cup cream
2 onions, chopped
butter
sherry

Sauté the onions in butter. Add the fiddleheads. Stir and toss a minute or two. Add the chicken broth. Bring to a boil, then drop to a simmer and cook for 30 to 40 minutes. Add the sherry—a mere tablespoon will give an extra dimension to this soup. Add the cream slowly. Stir and do not boil. Salt and pepper to taste. Serves 6.

FIDDLEHEAD SALAD

2 cups cooked fiddleheads
½ cup oil-and-vinegar dressing
1 cup sliced cherry tomatoes

Toss lightly while the fiddleheads are still warm from cooking. Serve on lettuce leaves. Serves 4 to 6.

I'd take a pot of basil growing on my window sill to any herb I can think of. Some years my seeds don't sprout, and then I'm out looking for the wild variety. It is not so heady, but it will do in a culinary pinch.

Wild basil grows in woods and along byways throughout the northern United States. The leaves grow opposite each other and are oval, pointed, and slightly toothed. Both leaves and stems are noticeably hairy. The blossoms are lavender.

My daughter has devised a fresh tomato sauce for spaghetti that uses lavish amounts of fresh basil. It may be served either at room temperature or heated through.

FRESH TOMATO SAUCE

4 tomatoes, chopped
2 tablespoons olive oil
salt and pepper to taste
½ cup fresh wild basil leaves, chopped
1 clove garlic, pressed

You might want to remove the skins from the tomatoes. To do so, drop each tomato into boiling water, count to five, and remove. The skins slip off easily. Blend all the ingredients in your blender or use a food processor. Serve over hot spaghetti. Sprinkle with Parmesan cheese. Serves 4.

MARINARA SAUCE

1 cup olive oil
1 cup fresh wild basil leaves, chopped
1 cup parsley, chopped
6 cloves garlic, pressed
pinch salt
1 teaspoon fresh ground pepper

Work all the ingredients into the olive oil. Store in the freezer. It will keep for months.

This sauce has a great many uses. We like it over linguine with a sprinkle of lemon juice and another of Parmesan cheese. Here's another variation, a nearly instant supper.

CLAM SAUCE WITH WILD BASIL

3 heaped tablespoons marinara sauce
1 can clams
½ cup dry vermouth
1 handful parsley, chopped

Cook all the ingredients together except the parsley and serve over pasta. The cooking process should take no more than 5 minutes. Sprinkle with parsley when you serve the plates. Serves 4.

My own children were crazy for picking cattails when they were very young, and we made many excursions to marshes, mucking about in rubber boots. What I didn't realize then was that nearly every part of the plant is edible: use the pollen in place of saffron, grind the roots for flour, and eat the young shoots in salad. This is an emergency plant for famine or a great depression. It is also the source for rushing chairs.

CHAIR RUSHING

Gather the rushes close to the roots in the summer. Take only the longest leaves. Tie in bunches and hang from the rafters to dry.

CATTAIL SHOOTS

Harvest the shoots in early spring. Wash. Boil in salted water. Drain. Serve with melted butter.

Day lilies are escapes from cultivated gardens, often found growing wild along roadsides in the county. Use the lilies at the bud stage.

STIR-FRIED DAY LILY BUDS

2 cups day lily buds
3 scallions, chopped
2 tablespoons peanut oil (scant)
1 clove garlic

Heat the oil in a wok. Add the garlic clove. When the oil is nearly smoking, remove the garlic and drop in the other ingredients. Stir the vegetables furiously over high heat for a couple of minutes. Remove and serve immediately on a hot platter. Season with any good soy sauce. 4 to 6 servings.

A north-woods Greek supper demands a wild grapevine growing close by. Wild grapes grow at the edge of the woods, reaching out toward the sun at the roadside. Gather the leaves in early summer before they turn tough. We like stuffed grape leaves (dolmas) for an appetizer, at room temperature with wine, or hot as a main dish.

STUFFED GRAPE LEAVES

several dozen grape leaves
1 cup rice (approximate)
1 pound ground chuck or lamb
salt and pepper
good pinch oregano
good pinch basil
1 large can tomatoes
lemon slices

Rinse the grape leaves to rid them of dust. Mix the meat and rice together; add salt and pepper and herbs. Put an approximate teaspoon of this mixture into the center of each leaf, with the stem end pointing towards you. Turn each side inward and roll from the stem end toward the top. Do this loosely to allow the rice to expand while cooking. Place in the bottom of a heavy casserole, stem side down. Slip thin lemon slices between each layer of grape leaves. Pour tomatoes (or tomato juice) over the top, making certain there is enough liquid to cook the rice. Cover and put in a 350-degree oven. Bake for approximately 1 hour. Remove with care. This amount should serve 8.

What the Greeks did for grape leaves, other cultures have done for the lowly cabbage. Here's a Scandinavian way to stuff cabbage leaves.

STUFFED CABBAGE LEAVES

1 medium-sized cabbage
¾ cup cooked rice
⅓ pound ground beef
⅓ pound ground pork
1 egg, beaten
1 teaspoon salt
good pinch white pepper

For cooking them:
butter
1 tablespoon brown sugar
2 cups broth

Boil or steam the cabbage until the leaves separate easily. Drain well. Discard the outer, tough leaves. Remove the leaves and trim off the tough center vein. Mix the rice, meats, egg, salt, and pepper in a bowl. Put approximately 2 tablespoons of mixture on each open leaf. Roll as you would grape leaves. Fasten with a toothpick if you must, and brown each leaf in butter in a heavy pot. Sprinkle brown sugar over the leaves and pour in the broth. Cover and simmer for 1½ hours, until tender. 6 generous servings.

Of all the wild green plants that have appeared on our table, the only one I can consistently sell the children on is asparagus. Like mushrooms, asparagus seem to pop up overnight. I sometimes think I could watch one grow if only I had the patience to lie down beside a tip pushing through the undergrowth and give the day to that calm pursuit.

I've found the best wild asparagus patches by walking or biking back roads in early fall. I look for long, spindly, sand-colored stalks with a few red berries clinging to the branches. These I mark down on an old map, and the next June I begin the search with map in hand, children in tow. The prime hunting time is the first clear day after after a heavy downpour.

Asparagus patches are top secrets to old foragers. I was given my first patch by someone who was leaving the county forever. He also provided me with a helpful clue—asparagus often grows beneath telephone lines, thanks to the birds. Think that one over. It makes sense.

When asparagus is in season, we like to make a meal of it with hollandaise sauce and a loaf of homemade bread for mopping up the plates.

DOOR COUNTY ASPARAGUS

1 pound asparagus
salt
water

Snap off the asparagus stems where they do so easily with no pressure. Bring water to a boil in a shallow pan. Lay in the asparagus and cook until just tender. Drain and serve immediately with the sauce.

There are many complicated recipes for making hollandaise sauce. This is the simplest I know. I've not had a failure on this one yet.

HOLLANDAISE SAUCE

2 egg yolks
¼ teaspoon salt
pinch cayenne pepper
½ cup melted butter
1 tablespoon fresh lemon juice

Beat the yolks until thick and lemon colored. Add the salt and cayenne. Add ¼ cup of the melted butter, 1 teaspoon at a time, beating all the while. Then combine the rest of the butter with the lemon juice and add 2 teaspoons at a time, again beating all the while.

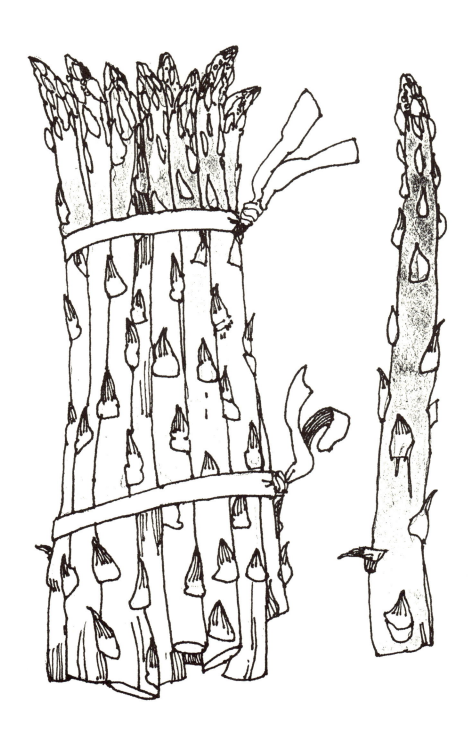

ASPARAGUS VINAIGRETTE

Cook the asparagus until just tender. Plunge immediately into cold water to preserve color and firmness. Pour your favorite vinegar and oil dressing over the asparagus.

ASPARAGUS SALAD SUPREME

bunch wild asparagus
½ cup homemade mayonnaise
½ cup sour half-and-half
pimentos

Cook the asparagus until just tender. Plunge into cold water and drain. Arrange on your best platter, spraying out the tips as if you were arranging a bouquet. Combine the mayonnaise and sour half-and-half. Pour a ribbon of sauce across the asparagus. Make a clever garnish with the red pimento.

WILD ASPARAGUS PIE

1 baked pie crust
1½ pounds asparagus
1 cup béchamel sauce (white sauce)
1 handful Swiss cheese, grated

Cut the asparagus into 3-inch slices. Steam quickly. Put the asparagus into the shell. Pour sauce over it. Sprinkle on the cheese. Bake in 350-degree oven until the cheese is brown and just crusting on the top.

BÉCHAMEL SAUCE

2 tablespoons butter
2 tablespoons flour
1 cup milk
good pinch salt
pinch white pepper or cayenne pepper
dash of sherry

Heat the milk. Do not let it form a skin on top. Melt the butter in a heavy-bottomed sauce pan. Do not let it brown. Add the flour with a wire whisk until it is perfectly blended. Mix in the milk quickly, beating all the while. Bring to a boil. Drop to a simmer and cook for about 5 minutes. Add the salt and pepper. Add the sherry. Cook a minute longer.

Note: Making this sauce scares off many beginning cooks. If you plan on a lifetime of cooking, it is well worth donating several rounds of ingredients to learning the process.

I once came upon a Texan camping in a Colorado alpine meadow. He had picked three huge bouquets of wild blue columbine, the state flower and protected by law. Texans have the reputation for doing things in a big way. This one had outdone himself.

A moral lies here. When foraging wild things, take care to leave enough in each patch for future growth. Mushrooms are the one exception, for the number you gather has no bearing on the next year's yield. Also, be sure to ask permission when gathering on private property.

The sugar maples that line the side roads are among the glories of the county. A few diligent souls are still making syrup. The price is dear, and why wouldn't it be? Almost 40 quarts of sap go into making one quart of syrup.

The pioneers learned to tap trees from the Indians, who cut a *V*-shaped gash in the maple, drained out sap, and boiled it, presumably with hot stones in the containers, to reduce the sap. The early settlers used wooden spiles to tap the trees and let the sap drip into wooden buckets. They then boiled off the sap in large iron caldrons. Today, most syrup makers have streamlined methods for extracting both sap and syrup, and the wooden sugar buckets have become prized collectibles.

Maple syrup will do anything that honey or brown sugar can do, and in a more subtle way. The Christmas present I'd like most from Door County (short of spending Christmas there) is several gallons of syrup. I wouldn't hoard it for Sunday breakfasts—I'd use it on biscuits, oatmeal, and pancakes throughout the year. Here are two simple desserts made extraordinary with maple syrup.

MAPLE GRAPEFRUIT

Slice grapefruits, taking care to cut each segment free but leaving it in its place. Dribble the grapefruits with Door County maple syrup and place under the broiler for a couple minutes, until the syrup has soaked in and the grapefruit is heated through. Good for breakfast in winter or after supper anytime.

DRIED-FRUIT COMPOTE

1 bag mixed dried fruit
lemon slices
1 cup yogurt
maple syrup

Put the contents of the bag of mixed dried fruit into a large jar. Mix in the slices of a lemon cut very thin. Add water to cover. Let sit several days, until the fruit is plump and tender. Spoon plain yogurt over the individual portions of compote and pass around the jug of maple syrup. A splash of brandy would not hurt the fruit in the "cooking" stage.

MAPLE SALAD DRESSING

1 egg yolk
¼ cup maple syrup
juice of ½ lemon
½ cup heavy cream, whipped

Beat the yolk and put it in a double boiler. Add the syrup and cook until thick. This should take only a minute or two. Let it cool and fold in the lemon juice and whipped cream. Serve over fresh fruit slices or a fruit salad. 4 servings.

MAPLE BAKED APPLES

8 Door County Courtlands
1 cup maple syrup
water
good pinch cardamom
pinch cinnamon

Core the apples but don't pierce the bottoms. Put them in a shallow baking dish. Fill the holes with maple syrup. Sprinkle on the spices. Add water to cover the bottom of the dish. Put in a 375-degree oven and bake until soft, basting with the juices.

MAPLE SYRUP CUSTARDS

4 eggs, beaten
3 cups milk
1 cup maple syrup
pinch salt
pinch nutmeg

Heat the milk but do not scald. Let cool slightly. Take a wire whip and thoroughly mix the eggs, milk, salt, and syrup. Pour the mixture into buttered glass custard cups and set them in a pan. Pour an inch of hot water into the pan. Sprinkle with nutmeg and put in a 350-degree oven. Bake 35 to 45 minutes. A knife that comes out clean when run around the edges of a custard means it is done. Cool on a cookie rack. Chill the custards.

The county is a haven for berry pickers. Having grown up among this breed, I recognize their colors. Every side road in summer is a possible patch. "Stop the car!" shrieks a picker, causing the driver to veer off the road and into a ditch. A berry-picking driver is even more dangerous and may roll into the face of oncoming traffic while intent on finding last year's raspberry bramble.

The common berries up here are wild strawberries, raspberries, thimbleberries, and blackberries. An educated eye can find gooseberries, partridgeberries, elderberries, serviceberries, and blueberries. Whichever berries one brings home, wild and wonderful treats can be made.

Al Johnson's Restaurant in Sister Bay serves a great raspberry pie. I wheedled this recipe from a grower in another part of the state. A subtle wild flavor underlies its natural sweetness.

WILD RASPBERRY PIE

1 baked pie shell
enough raspberries to nearly fill the shell
1½ cups raspberries, mashed
⅔ cup sugar
3 tablespoons cornstarch
1 cup water
pinch salt

Fill the crust with raspberries. Mash the remainder in a sauce pan. Add the sugar, cornstarch, water, and salt. Cook over low heat, stirring constantly until the mixture thickens. Pour over the berries in the crust, taking care to fill all the crevices. Put the pie in the icebox and leave it there for at least 4 hours, or overnight.

This pie deserves Wisconsin whipping cream. As you whip it, sweeten with only a touch of sugar and vanilla.

Thimbleberries bloom in June and produce berries ready for eating in very late July or early August. The berries grow on large bushes bearing huge leaves resembling grape leaves. The berry is an intense, ruddy red. Children love to pick them, for, true to their name, they fit like thimbles over the fingers. Salmonberry is their other name, not nearly as magical.

Last year we made jam. We also froze enough berries to make a sauce to serve with our Easter ham.

THIMBLEBERRY SAUCE

4 cups thimbleberries
½ cup water
1 cup sugar (heaped)
2 tablespoons cornstarch (scant)

Put the berries, sugar, and water into a pan and stir gently. Bring to a simmer. Mix the cornstarch with 8 tablespoons cold water. Add to the berries and stir. Simmer for a few minutes until the sauce thickens. Serve this sauce hot or cold. It is excellent over ice cream or waffles, lovely with ham or cold roasted chicken.

Wild strawberries must surely be the sweetest of all wild fruits. My favorite roadside patch, which offered several quarts each season, has been lost to "progress." For three years running, road crews sprinkled some evil-smelling dust to kill the weeds on either side of the road. The strawberries have disappeared for good, although the Queen Anne's lace, a chief offender, has come back stronger than before.

If you find wild strawberries in profusion, as we used to, you might want to jam some to bring back June days in the gray of winter. Use your favorite domestic pectin recipe, or try this old-fashioned way.

WILD STRAWBERRY JAM

4 cups berries, crushed
4 cups sugar (scant)
1 tablespoon lemon juice

Stir the berries and sugar in a large, heavy enameled pan. Bring to a boil very slowly. Stir gently and thoroughly and keep at a low boil for 14 minutes. Skim off the foam; sprinkle with lemon juice and allow to cool. Seal in sterilized jars by topping with melted paraffin.

STRAWBERRY LEAF TEA

A refreshing tea can be made with strawberry leaves and stems. Simply crush them in your hands, put them in a teapot, and pour boiling water over them. This is a fine source of vitamin C.

I'd walk a mile for a Door County blueberry. I've walked more than a few and usually to no avail. I've found bushes by the hundreds without a berry on them. Last year I lucked out and picked a cup. We ate them with sugar and cream. But I know they're down there in the southern Door, the secret blueberry patches hoarded by the secret pickers. When I find them I'll make the following.

WILD BLUEBERRY GRUNT

2 cups wild blueberries
1 cup water
½ cup sugar
1½ cups flour
2 teaspoons baking powder
⅛ teaspoon nutmeg
grated peel of ½ lemon
good pinch salt
¾ cup milk

Put the blueberries and water into an enamel-bottomed skillet. Stir in the sugar. Cook the berries until the mixture bubbles. Remove from the heat while you mix the flour, baking powder, rind, nutmeg, and salt in a small bowl. Stir in the milk very quickly to moisten the dry ingredients. A light hand here is imperative. Bring the blueberries back to a simmer and drop spoonfuls of dough on top of them. Cover the skillet and cook for 12 to 15 minutes. Do not peek! Serve the dumplings with the berry sauce. Pour heavy Wisconsin cream over each portion. Should serve 8.

You could cycle through Ireland during blackberry season eating berries from the hedgerows and never go hungry, for the crop is of overwhelming abundance. The same goes for the Oregon coast, where landowners often burn away brambles lest they take over their property. In Door County, blackberries are scarcer, and they are cherished.

This berry has everything to recommend it: it keeps well in its natural state; it cooks, cans, and freezes beautifully. And, as a true berry picker would understand, it makes a satisfying ping as it hits the pail. Some folks complain of seediness, but this is the case only after a long, dry summer. Blackberries ripen at the end of August, a month when you can generally count on lots of rain. Our family's first gathering always goes into cobbler.

BLACKBERRY COBBLER

Make your best shortcake dough. Here's a good one:

2 cups flour
4 teaspoons baking powder
½ teaspoon salt
1 tablespoon sugar
4 tablespoons butter
¾ cup milk

Filling:
6 cups blackberries
1 cup sugar
½ teaspoon cinnamon
melted butter

Sift the dry ingredients. With a pastry cutter, quickly work in the butter and then stir in the milk, little by little. Turn out on a floured board and form into one large cover for the cobbler pan. Or you may prefer dropping the mixture by spoonfuls on the berries.

Heat the berries and sugar in a pan until the sugar melts into the berries. Pour the mixture into a large baking dish. Sprinkle with cinnamon and pour a little melted butter over all. Place the dough on top; pour on a little more melted butter. Sprinkle with sugar and place in a 425-degree oven. Bake for about ½ hour and serve with cream.

Note: For a less substantial dish, use half the amount of biscuit dough and bake 20 to 25 minutes. This version is preferred by the blackberry fiends in our family.

The following is an old-fashioned "receipt" for a children's tonic. The old woman who gave it to me insists it's "good for what ails you" and especially fine for "summer complaint." The only complaint my children have in summer is that I don't haul them to the go-carts often enough, but I present the recipe for those who might make use of it for other reasons.

BLACKBERRY TONIC

½ pound sugar
½ pint white vinegar
½ teaspoon allspice
½ teaspoon ground cloves
¼ teaspoon ground nutmeg
2 quarts blackberries

Boil the sugar, vinegar, and spices together for at least fifteen minutes. Add the blackberries and simmer another fifteen minutes. Bottle in clean jars and store in the icebox.

Gooseberries are an old-fashioned fruit that many berry fanciers these days leave alone. While the picking is easy enough, cleaning off the prickles is a trouble. Nonetheless, I want the children to grow up with certain advantages, and one of these is eating gooseberry pie.

ONCE-A-YEAR GOOSEBERRY PIE

favorite double pie crust
¼ cup butter
1 cup brown sugar
2 eggs
3 tablespoons evaporated milk
2 cups gooseberries (heaped)

Cream the sugar and butter; beat in the eggs. Add the milk and gooseberries. Bake the bottom pie crust at 425 degrees for 3 minutes, just long enough to set it so the berry mixture won't make it mushy. Remove. Cool a few minutes, then pour in the filling. Fit on the top crust. Sprinkle on sugar. Bake 15 minutes, then lower the heat to 375 and bake for about a half hour longer. Remove and cool.

If I had my druthers, I'd spend the fall in Door County, watching the maples turn to flame. Leaves underfoot, leaves overhead, blue sky, blue water.

As a neighbor likes to say, it's the time of year when you can stop the car in the middle of Highway 42, flag down a friend who's going in the opposite direction, and just sit there and visit. It's the county exactly the way we want it, all for ourselves with no one else around to spoil our views.

Though I know better, I never think of autumn on the peninsula with a driving rain, the firewood sodden, and everything mildewing. My ideal is Indian summer followed by a cold snap that makes me feel so exhilarated that I want to cut wood, refinish furniture, and, like a squirrel, gather nuts and put them by. If I could beat the squirrels, I'd made bread or pie.

VIVIAN'S ORANGE BEECHNUT BREAD

2 cups flour
½ teaspoon salt
½ teaspoon baking soda
¾ cup sugar
¾ cup beechnuts, chopped
1 egg, beaten
¾ cup orange juice
2 tablespoons lemon juice
¼ teaspoon lemon rind, grated
2 tablespoons melted shortening

Sift the dry ingredients. Thoroughly combine the moist ingredients in a bowl. Add them to the dry ingredients. Do this with a light hand, until just mixed. Pour into a greased loaf pan and bake at 350 degrees for about 75 minutes. Cool on a rack before serving.

BEECHNUT PIE

single pie crust
1 cup beechnuts, chopped
3 eggs, beaten
¼ pound butter
1 cup corn syrup or maple syrup
¾ cup light brown sugar
good pinch salt

Cream the eggs and sugar. Add the other ingredients and pour into a half-baked pie shell. Bake the pie at 425 degrees for 15 minutes; then lower the heat to 375 degrees and bake for half an hour. Cool and serve with vanilla ice cream

A picnic in the pocket is a handy thing to have along on a hike through the woods in brisk fall weather. The meat pasty is famous for warming the hands and stomachs of Upper Michigan miners. It should do the same for Door County hikers. I pass on the recipe below as given to me by a Michigan native.

PASTIES

3 or 4 medium-sized potatoes, sliced thin
1 large onion, chopped
¾ pound flank steak, cubed
½ cup kidney suet
salt and pepper to taste
several tablespoons diced carrots (optional)
1 clove garlic, minced (optional)

Mix all the ingredients in a bowl, except for the suet. Roll out a double pie crust dough and cut into 6-inch circles. Put the meat and vegetable mixture on each, sprinkle on some suet, and fold over and crimp the edges. Prick the dough so steam may escape. Bake 30 minutes at 350 to 375 degrees.

Note: My Michigan friend tells me that garlic and carrots are never used by purists. I prefer the additional flavor. He also suggests making a huge batch when you finally go to the effort. Bake them all, freeze some, keep some in the refrigerator, he says. In the old days, Upper Michigan mothers used to mail them parcel post to sons and daughters in college.

ORCHARDS · AND · FIELDS

In the dead of winter, one of my travel fantasies is to be biking north through the peninsula with the cherry trees in bloom, starting at Sturgeon Bay and ending at the tip. To go by car is simpler, but then I'd need to stop, get out, and smell. By cycling the back roads, the wonderful assault on the senses would be constant. I'd have it forever like a Proustian cookie, tucked away and ready to be pulled out whenever I wanted its essence. And the same holds true for apple blossom time.

To own and work those orchards is another matter. The pruning, clearing, spraying, and nurturing must be figured in with the mental worry over crop failure due to weather catastrophes. I only hope the owners hold out, ready to gamble like true farmers for that proverbial one more year. When the orchards go down, the prospect of condominiums marching up the county one by one will loom as a dark possibility.

Surely, there is nothing sweeter than a stolen cherry or a stolen green apple. Stealing fruit is part of a small-town childhood ethic that grown-ups seem to forget. The meanest old ladies (and pardon the chauvinistic slip) were always the ones to get robbed when I was a child, my own grandmother among them. These were also the ladies who didn't give treats on Halloween. For a child to escape with a few cherries or apples in a baseball cap was a rite of passage that I suspect still goes on today. My children, with a parcel of other grammar school friends, were chased from a field by a furious orchardman, reportedly with a shotgun in his hand.

Admittedly, there are more honorable ways to get fruit in season. We watch the cherries ripen day by day, and just before the mechanical shakers come in, the Pick Your Own signs crop up. It's lazy picking, for we needn't strip a tree. We go from one overladen branch to another, pulling off the fruit into a bucket.

We think the Viking Orchard cherries are the sweetest of all, but that's sentimental nonsense, for we simply like the owners and their beautiful red barn.

We collect with the Viking buckets and take the cherries home in our old scrub pails and whatever boilers we can round up. If we can't start cooking or preserving right away, we cover the cherries with cold well water which "holds" them until the children start pitting.

For this is children's work. I may let them run off on dirty dishes but not on cherry pitting. Among the products of Yankee ingenuity and Victorian invention are a plethora of cherry pitters. I find my children's fingers still work best.

These sour Montmorencies are sweet enough to eat hand to mouth, and they preserve with an astounding color, like liquid rubies.

Our need for this fruit is simple: the children, who adore cherries, are rigorous in their demands for the same old favorites.

DOOR COUNTY CHERRY PIE

favorite double pie crust
2 heaped cups pitted cherries
½ cup cherry juice
1 cup sugar
1½ teaspoon flour
pinch salt
beaten egg white

Roll out the bottom crust and brush with beaten egg white to prevent sogginess. Mix the filling and put in the pie crust. Cover the top with a latticed crust. Dust with sugar and cinnamon if you wish. Bake in a 450-degree oven for 10 minutes, then reduce the heat to 350 degrees and bake close to 30 minutes longer. Remove and cool on a rack.

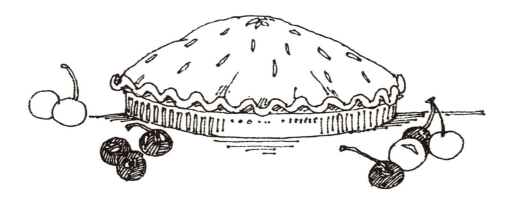

We use the small, flat old granite pie pans for cherry pie, hence the reduced amount of cherries as noted above. I save the extra dough for children to make tarts with when cherries are in abundance.

CHERRY TARTS

leftover pie dough
1 cup cherries
½ cup sugar
good pinch flour
¼ cup cherry juice (scant)
beaten egg white

Roll out the dough and cut circles with a wide-mouthed jar lid. Put the filling in the center and brush the egg white around the edges. Fit on the top crust and crimp the crusts together with your fingers to seal. Prick the top with a fork or slit with a sharp knife to allow steam to escape while cooking. Put the tarts on a cookie sheet. Dust with sugar and cinnamon and bake at 375 degrees for 25 to 30 minutes.

EASY CHERRY COBBLER

1 can Door County cherry pie filling
⅓ cup butter
¼ cup brown sugar
1 cup flour, sifted
1 teaspoon cinnamon
½ cup chopped walnuts (optional)

Pour the pie filling into a buttered baking dish. Blend the butter, sugar, flour, and cinnamon with a pastry cutter until crumbly. Add the walnuts. Sprinkle the topping over the cherries. Bake about 20 minutes in a 400-degree oven, until the crumbs are golden. Remove and cool. Serve with heavy cream or vanilla ice cream.

Cherry bounce may have as many recipes are there are devotees. Here is one from an anonymous giver who does not drink under ordinary circumstances. However, given cherry season and a good crop, he might make bounce. He figures a few cherries after supper on winter evenings can't hurt him.

CHERRY BOUNCE

3 pounds Door County cherries
1 fifth brandy
½ pound sugar

Wash the cherries. Put them in a large, wide-mouthed jar. A commercial-sized mayonnaise jar will do nicely. Pour the brandy over them and screw on the lid. Put aside in a warm place and forget about it for 2 months. At the end of this time, pour off the brandy and mix it with a syrup made of heating the sugar with a half cup of water until just dissolved. Pour this brandy syrup over the cherries, fasten the lid, and leave them another 2 or 3 weeks before eating.

SUMMER CHERRY SOUP

½ cup seedless raisins
several thin slices of orange
several thin slices of lemon
1 stick cinnamon
2 cups water
1 teaspoon lemon juice
4 cups pitted cherries
¾ to 1 cup sugar
dash salt
1½ tablespoons cornstarch
whipped cream

Simmer the first six ingredients for 20 minutes. Remove the cinnamon stick. Add the cherries, salt, and sugar. While the soup comes to a boil, mix the cornstarch with a little water and stir in quickly. Cook for 10 minutes. Cool, then chill. Serve with slightly sweetened whipped cream on top.

MARION'S CHERRY RHUBARB DESSERT

1 cup flour
1 cup brown sugar
1 cup quick oatmeal
½ cup butter, melted

Mix these ingredients and press into a 9-by-13-inch pan, reserving a cup of this mix for topping. topping.

3 cups fresh, pitted cherries
¾ cup sugar
3 tablespoons tapioca

Cook these ingredients until thick. Cool.

1 cup sugar
1 cup water
2 tablespoons cornstarch
1 teaspoon vanilla

Cook these ingredients until thick and clear. Take 4 cups of diced rhubarb and spread over the bottom crust. Mix the cherries with the syrup and pour over the rhubarb. Sprinkle the topping over all and bake in a 350-degree oven for 45 minutes. Serve warm with whipped cream.

Of all the Door County apples, Courtlands and Winesaps are my favorites for their versatility. Like Jonathans, they're "keepers," and I don't have to worry about them turning soft in a week or so. Surely a part of the joy of eating apples is the hard crunch and spurt of flavor between one's teeth. This means autumn to me as surely as spying wild geese flying south.

If you prefer apples tree ripened, watch for the Pick Your Own signs. Among my favorites was one that appeared year after year at harvest time near Egg Harbor along Highway 42. It read, Aples, 1 buck, 1 bu. At some point that 1 buck was changed to 2, and now the sign has disappeared altogether.

Still, apples remain a bargain up here. A small-sized family ought to be able to pick enough in an hour to last the winter. If I had several bushels of Courtlands, here's what I'd do with them.

DRYING APPLES

Core and peel the apples. Slice them. Dry on screens in a balmy place until dry. Turn often so that the surfaces get air. String the dried apples on heavy thread with a rug needle and hang. Pull off as needed. A foolproof way to dry apples in Wisconsin humidity is to use a commercial drier. Consult an organic-gardening journal for price and where to find one.

SUZY'S APPLE CRISP

1 cup flour
1 cup sugar
1 teaspoon baking powder
1 teaspoon salt
1 egg
5 apples peeled and sliced
½ cup butter

Dust the apples with a quarter of the sugar and some cinnamon. Put them in a buttered 9-by-5 bread loaf pan. Sift the dry ingredients. Add the egg. Mix together. The mixture will be dry and crumbly. Put it over the apples. Pour the melted butter over the top, taking care to spread it evenly. Bake at 350 degrees for half an hour. Serve warm with whipped cream. Serves 6.

COURTLAND APPLE PIE

Crust:
2¼ cups sifted unbleached flour
1 teaspoon salt
¼ cup water
¾ cup shortening or lard

Mix the flour and salt in a bowl. Remove ⅓ cup of the flour and mix quickly with the water in a cup. Add the shortening to the dry flour: cut in with a pastry cutter until the mixture is like peas. Add the water and flour paste and mix together until it adheres; just a few minutes should to it. A light hand is imperative if you wish a light crust. Put the dough aside while you fix the filling. A 20-minute rest will allow the gluten to work.

Apple filling:
enough peeled and sliced apples to fill a 9-inch pie plate
½ cup currants
pinch salt
¾ cup sugar
teaspoon cinnamon (scant)
butter
juice from ½ lemon (use only if you don't have a tart apple)
good pinch flour

Preheat the oven to 450 degrees. Mix the filling together. Roll out the bottom crust. Put in the filling. Roll out the top crust and cut a design of air holes in it with a fork. Dot the apples with bits of butter and fit on the top crust, crimping it together. Sprinkle the pie with cinnamon and sugar and put in the oven. Bake at 450 degrees for 10 minutes; lower the temperature to 375 degrees and bake another 35 minutes. Remove and cool on a rack. This pie takes nicely to a wedge of Wisconsin cheddar.

DOOR COUNTY APPLE BUTTER

2 dozen apples
1 cup water
1 cup cider vinegar

Core and pare the apples into a large pot containing the water and vinegar. Do not use an aluminum pot. Cook to a mush. Put through a strainer or a food processor. Add the sugar or honey to taste as you would with applesauce. Put back into the pot and add the following spices:

2 tablespoons cinnamon
1½ teaspoons ground cloves
½ teaspoon allspice
½ teaspoon nutmeg
good pinch salt

Simmer the butter over a very low heat, stirring frequently. Add more water if necessary to avoid scorching. When the butter sheets from a spoon, pour it into sterilized jars and seal. Makes about 8 cups.

APPLE CHUTNEY

3 large green tomatoes, diced
1 tablespoon salt
1½ cups brown sugar
4½ cups cider vinegar
20 tart apples, diced
2½ cups seedless raisins
1 large red onion, sliced
1 knob of ginger root, sliced fine
8 scallions, sliced
1 large clove garlic, diced fine
½ teaspoon cayenne pepper
3 tablespoons mustard seed

Put the tomatoes in a wide, flat dish and sprinkle with salt. Leave overnight. Drain the next day. Heat the vinegar and sugar in a large enameled kettle to dissolve the sugar. Add all the ingredients and cook slowly, stirring often for about 45 minutes or until the fruit is soft and the volume reduced. Put in sterilized jars and seal. Makes about 8 cups.

For this tart you need a French tart pan with a removable bottom. This is an extremely handsome dessert to present to company, but it cannot compare to good old-fashioned American apple pie.

FRENCH APPLE TART

dough for single crust
5 Courtland apples, peeled and sliced
½ cup sugar
apple peelings
brandy or calvados
butter

Butter a tart pan and put the dough in it. Dust the bottom lightly with sugar. Arrange the apple slices in a swirling circle; sugar them and arrange another layer until all the apples are used. Butter the top lightly and bake in a 375-degree oven for half an hour. The apples should be slightly browned on the surface. Remove. Make a glaze by cooking the apple peelings with a bit of sugar, water, and brandy. Pour this over the top when the tart has cooled. Serve with a jug of heavy cream or on its own.

COUNTRY FRIED APPLES

I use this recipe to stretch a supper when friends drop in unexpectedly. Fried apples marry well with a main dish such as roasted chicken or ham.

Door County apples
butter
brown sugar

Heat some butter and a very little bit of oil in a heavy iron skillet. Slice the apples off the core into the frying pan. Brown and turn, meanwhile adding a sprinkle of brown sugar. Serve hot.

LAZY APPLESAUCE

Courtlands or other tart apples
honey
cinnamon

This is the quickest and the best applesauce I know. Cut the apples off the core into a large, heavy pot. Add just a bit of water to the bottom of the pot so the apples won't scorch as you begin cooking them. When the pot is nearly full, cover and bring to a boil. Push the apples around while they're cooking. When they begin to get mushy, help them out by mashing them. Puree them after cooking, either in a blender or a food processor. Add honey and cinnamon to taste. Freeze or store in the icebox.

The following two recipes are best made with home-cooked applesauce, for the flavor is always superior to "store bought."

SWEDISH APPLE CAKE

1½ cups applesauce
2 cups zwieback crumbs or crumbled, stale limpa
4 tablespoons butter

Melt the butter in a large, heavy skillet. Add the breadcrumbs and stir until golden brown. Butter a baking dish and put in crumbs and applesauce in alternating layers, ending with crumbs. Bake in a 375-degree oven for half an hour. Cool and serve with cream or vanilla sauce. Serves 6.

VANILLA SAUCE

1 cup light cream
3 egg yolks
3 tablespoons sugar
pinch salt
1 teaspoon vanilla extract
1 cup whipped cream (optional)

Beat the egg yolks and sugar in the top of a double boiler. Heat the light cream and add to the yolks in a thin stream, beating all the while. Cook until thick, stirring constantly. Remove from the heat and continue to stir while you add the vanilla and salt. Just before serving, fold in the whipped cream.

APPLE NUT BREAD

Several slices of this bread provide a healthy breakfast for children or adults in too big a hurry for a proper meal.

1¼ cups applesauce
1 cup brown sugar
2 eggs
1½ cups sifted unbleached flour
¼ cup wheat germ
1 teaspoon baking soda
1 teaspoon soda
1½ teaspoons salt
1 teaspoon cinnamon (scant)
½ teaspoon nutmeg
⅓ cup melted shortening
1½ cups rolled oats
1 cup seedless raisins
½ cup finely chopped walnuts

Beat together the sugar and eggs; add the applesauce and beat again. Sift together the dry ingredients except for the oatmeal and add to the egg mixture. Blend quickly. Stir in the shortening, oats, raisins, and nuts. Pour into a well-buttered loaf pan and bake 1 hour at 350 degrees. Cool before slicing.

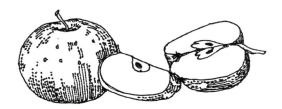

APPLE PASTRY BARS

This recipe, from Marion Metzer, is Danish in origin.

2½ cups flour, sifted
1 teaspoon salt
1 cup shortening
1 egg yolk
milk
2 cups cornflakes
8 cups tart apples, pared and sliced
½ to ¾ cup sugar
1 teaspoon cinnamon
⅛ teaspoon nutmeg
1 egg white

Combine the flour and salt in a bowl. Cut in the shortening. Beat the egg yolk in a 1-cup measure and add enough milk to make ⅔ cup. Stir the egg mixture into the flour mixture. Roll out half of the pastry on a floured surface to measure 12-by-17 inches. Line a 10½-by-15½-by-1-inch baking pan with the pastry. Sprinkle with the cornflakes. Top with the apples. Combine the sugar, cinnamon, and nutmeg. Sprinkle over the apples. Roll the remaining pastry and place over the apples. Seal the edges. Cut slits on top for steam to escape. Beat the egg white until frothy and brush on the pastry. Bake in a 375-degree oven about 50 minutes. Drizzle powdered sugar glaze over the pastry while still warm. Cut into bars.

DOOR COUNTY CHERRY BARS

Instead of apples, substitute

3 cups fresh pitted cherries
¾ cup sugar
3 tablespoons tapioca

Cook these ingredients until thick. Allow to cool and use the pastry recipe as given.

The apple recipes could go on forever. But when we get tired of eating apples, I hoard the rest away in the cellar, each one wrapped with care in old tissue. For the plain truth is that one rotten apple will spoil the whole barrel.

Roadside stands are another feast, and like farmers' markets, so seductive that I generally take home more than I'd planned. I want everything in sight—a heaping bucket of new potatoes and all the string beans I can stuff in the car. I'll take one of those wastebaskets too, the one made of pink-and-yellow egg cartons with shells glued up and down the sides, and for the trip home, cram it full of sweet corn.

These Midwest institutions are often the simplest of operations: a table set on sawhorses, with a coffee can to make your own change. Presume an honest public and you'll find it so. The Neil Teskie family has been operating on this premise for years and sells out its produce daily in season.

Surely, the ultimate in roadside stands is Koepsel's, located on Highway 57 between Bailey's Harbor and Sister Bay. Where else but in Wisconsin could you

88 ORCHARDS AND FIELDS

find fur coats among the broccoli and cabbages, a full-fledged bakery, and a case full of cheeses and sausages? Bea Landin's Ho-Made Products can be purchased at Koepsel's if you miss her place in Gills Rock.

Then there's the barn stuffed full of antiques, primitives, Victorian walnut and oak, along with the best cache of decoys in the county. Buy a kraut cutter and a few of the Koepsel's red cabbages and apples and you have the makings for a lovely mess.

DANISH RED CABBAGE

1 onion, chopped fine
4 cups shredded red cabbage
2 apples, sliced fine
3 tablespoons vinegar
good pinch caraway seeds
salt and pepper to taste
several spoons bacon fat
2 tablespoons brown sugar

Sauté the onion in bacon fat on low heat. Add the sugar and cook a minute or so longer. Add the rest of the ingredients and cook very slowly, turning and stirring often until tender. If the liquid evaporates, add a bit of red wine to moisten. Serves 6 modestly. This dish is traditionally served in fall and winter, but it tastes very good indeed on one of those crisp August evenings when the temperature in the county has dropped to the 40s.

If you should find yourself, as I have, with a kitchen full of vegetables that you bought for their sheer beauty and bounty, or better yet, that you grew yourself in the county's short season, you might want to make a vegetable stew. This stew will swallow nearly any vegetable you can find to put into it. It gathers flavor by sitting overnight and tastes good either hot or cold. I find it addictive myself and suitable for a midnight snack. It will feed a hungry crowd and cooks best in a heavy cocotte.

BOUNTY STEW FOR POOR POETS AND FRIENDS

A mess of vegetables such as:
carrots
green beans
peas
cauliflower
celery
zucchini
tomatoes
sweet onions
new potatoes in skins
corn off the cob
mushrooms
green peppers
olive oil
garlic, several buds
brown rice
water
Tabasco sauce
salt
parsley, finely chopped

Scrub the vegetables and chop them into bite-sized pieces. Take a big pot and dump in the vegetables as you go. Drizzle over the top about ¾ cup olive oil (no need to use the virgin oil, which is very mild; this stew profits from the cheaper, everyday quality) add at least a cup of brown rice and at least two cups of water. Mix well together with your hands. Add a healthy tablespoon of salt and several shakes of Tabasco sauce. Mix again. At the last mixing, include parsley and several buds of garlic that have been peeled and finely minced. Bring to a boil on the stove, then put in a medium oven, around 350 degrees. Cook until the rice is done. this will probably take 1 to 1½ hours.

I like to serve this stew to Door County visitors I suspect may have become vegetarians since I last saw them. I serve it with my favorite French bread, and a pox on them if they no longer eat white unbleached flour. I serve the bread with Lake to Lake butter, which is made right in the county.

I like Julia Child. Who can resist her with all that verve and genial knowledge? But I find her recipe for French bread absurd for the American housewife. It takes nearly two whole pages in her cookbook and a good long time to prepare. I do not try baking bread in Door County when the humidity is high and the barometer is dropping. Bread, like popovers, is not interested in rising in that kind of weather, and you're better off going straight to the grocery to find whatever you can.

EASY FRENCH BREAD

1 envelope dried yeast
1 heaping teaspoon sugar
2 cups warm water
2 teaspoons salt
4 cups plus unbleached white flour

Put the yeast in a large bowl. Add the salt, sugar, and water. Mix well and allow the yeast to work for several minutes. Gradually mix in the flour until the mixture is fairly firm. Flour your hands and knead the dough for close to 10 minutes. This is the crucial aspect in making bread. The air must get into the mixture, and if you don't know how to knead, take a lesson from a home baker who does. Grease the dough lightly and put in a bowl; cover with a damp, clean dish towel and let it rise for an hour in a warm corner of the kitchen. Grease a cookie sheet and sprinkle with cornmeal. Punch down the dough when it has nearly doubled in bulk and work into two narrow loaves. Place them on the cookie sheet diagonally and cut quick diagonal slits down each loaf with a very sharp knife. Let the loaves rise about 40 minutes. Brush them lightly with melted butter. (Margarine will *not* make a good crust.) Bake the bread on the middle rack of a preheated 450-degree oven for 7 minutes; reduce the heat to 375 degrees and bake another 35 to 40 minutes. A shallow pan of boiling water placed on the bottom rack will produce a splendid crust. Serve this bread the day you make it or freeze it until needed.

Another sort of roadside attraction I've found on a back road in the upper Door is a stand announcing free vegetables for passersby. Such down-home generosity is remarkable in the latter part of this century. But even with a short growing season, some gardeners produce more than they can eat or put by. Here are several recipes that should use up any extra vegetables you might grow or find on your back door stoop, the first three of them based on Door County immigrant cookery.

MASHED TURNIPS

3 medium-sized turnips
3 medium-sized potatoes
3 tablespoons butter
1 teaspoon sugar
salt and white pepper to taste
½ cup cream or rich milk

Wash, peel, and dice the vegetables. Cook the turnips in salted water about half an hour, then add the potatoes and cook until soft. Drain. Mash or put through a potato ricer. Heat the cream or milk and beat into the vegetables. Add the butter and beat again. Season to taste with sugar, salt, and pepper. Serve with pork sausages for a simple supper. Serves 6.

BEAUTIFUL BEETS

6 beets
2 tablespoons butter
salt and white pepper
sprig dillweed, chopped
dash lemon juice

Scrub and boil the beets in salted water until tender. It might take nearly an hour. Reserve ½ cup of beet liquid. Peel and slice the beets and return to the pot. Add the butter and dill and simmer a few minutes. Season to taste with salt, pepper, and lemon juice. Serve in individual glass bowls. Serves 6.

PICKLED CUCUMBERS

3 small, young cucumbers
½ cup vinegar
2 tablespoons water
1 tablespoon sugar
good pinch salt
pinch white pepper
1 tablespoon parsley, chopped

Cucumbers from the garden need not be peeled, as their skins are tender and sweet. Slice them fine and lay in a wide, flat bowl. Mix the dressing and pour it over the cucumbers. Let them rest in the dressing all afternoon in a cool place. Serves 6.

ZUCCHINI STEW

10 zucchini, sliced
several handfuls mushrooms, sliced
⅓ cup butter
2 tablespoons flour
2 cloves garlic, cut lengthwise
1 small sprig fresh dillweed
2 cups sour cream
salt and pepper

Put the zucchini, garlic, and dillweed in a sauce pan. Cover with salted boiling water. Cook very quickly for just a few minutes so that the squash is still firm. Drain. Reserve ¼ cup of the cooking liquid. Sauté the mushrooms in butter in a large, heavy skillet. Stir in the flour with care, stirring the whole while. Add the zucchini, liquid, and sour cream. Simmer the whole mess 5 minutes. Salt and pepper to taste. Serve over wild rice or with buttered noodles. 12 servings.

ZUCCHINI AND YELLOWNECK SALAD

5 small zucchini
5 small yellowneck squash
oil-and-vinegar dressing
1 teaspoon chopped dillweed

Take your sharpest French knife and slice the squash on the diagonal in very thin slices. Toss with a dressing made of 1 part salad vinegar and 2 parts olive oil, a pinch of dry mustard, and salt and pepper. Sprinkle on the dillweed and toss again. Marinate several hours in the icebox. Toss again and serve. 6 to 8 servings.

CORN OR ZUCCHINI FRITTERS

1 cup flour
1 teaspoon baking powder
½ teaspoon salt
½ teaspoon sugar
1 egg, beaten
⅓ cup milk
1 tablespoon melted shortening
1⅔ cup fresh corn off the cob or finely chopped zucchini
vegetable oil

Mix the egg, milk, and shortening. Sift the dry ingredients. Add wet to dry and beat quickly and lightly. Add the corn or zucchini. Heat an inch of oil nearly to the smoking point in a heavy, deep frying pan. Drop in several spoonfuls of batter, taking care not to overcrowd the pan. Fry quickly, turning just once. Drain on paper and serve immediately. 6 servings.

STIR-FRIED ZUCCHINI

4 medium zucchini
1 clove garlic
1 tablespoon peanut oil

Grate the zucchini. Put in linen dish towels and squeeze out the moisture. Heat the oil in a wok until nearly smoking. Put in the garlic clove. Wait a minute and then remove the garlic. Drop in the zucchini by handfuls and stir furiously for 2 minutes. Serve immediately. 6 servings.

If it's a good year for the resort business, it will mean a good year for tomatoes. For tomatoes, like tourists, thrive on sunny days in Door County. If we should have tomatoes in profuse abundance, here is what we do with some of them.

FRESH TOMATO SOUP

6 or 7 tomatoes
3 scallions
½ teaspoon salt
½ teaspoon pepper
pinch sugar
pinch marjoram
pinch thyme
pinch basil
2 tablespoons lemon juice
1 cup chicken broth
yogurt
chopped parsley

Peel and slice the tomatoes. Seed them if you wish. We don't bother. Mince the scallions. Put all the ingredients except the broth, yogurt, and parsley into a blender. Blend to a puree. Put the blended ingredients with the broth into a large pot. Bring to a boil. Simmer just a few minutes and remove. Cool the soup and refrigerate it. When you serve it, garnish with a dollop of yogurt and some chopped parsley. 6 to 8 servings. This soup is marvelous for a cool lunch on a hot, steamy day.

FRIED GREEN TOMATOES

This is my all-time favorite tomato side dish, excellent with Wisconsin bratwursts and boiled new potatoes.

green tomatoes
1 egg
water
flour or fine breadcrumbs
oil

Slice green tomatoes one-half-inch thick. Beat the egg and add a few drops of water to it. Heat oil in a large, heavy skillet until very hot but not smoking. Dip the tomatoes in egg and then dredge them in flour. Fry until crisp and golden on the outside and hot and juicy on the inside. Drain on paper towels and serve right away.

JULIE'S LASAGNE

My eleven-year-old daughter devised this dish for supper one night. It was a grand surprise to her family and to the assembled guests, all of whom were fairly competent in the kitchen.

2 cups fresh tomato puree
salt and pepper to taste
2 cloves garlic, chopped fine
½ teaspoon oregano
½ teaspoon basil
½ pound broad noodles
¾ pound mozzarella cheese, sliced thin

Make a puree of 6 tomatoes by blanching, peeling, and chopping them, and putting them through a food processor or into a blender. Butter a shallow baking dish. Mix the puree with the garlic, herbs, salt, and pepper. Cook the noodles. Make layers of tomato puree, cheese, and noodles. Cover and bake in a 350-degree oven for 30 minutes. Remove the cover; let brown 5 minutes. Remove from the oven and serve hot. 6 servings.

TOMATOES FOR DESSERT

If you find yourself with a bunch of ripe tomatoes, you might like to try this old-fashioned dessert. Peel the tomatoes. Slice and sugar them. Chill an hour and serve in your best crystal dishes.

We like a sour dill pickle with our Door County smoked fish. Being unable to find our favorite kosher style here, we decided to make our own. We like to think it's our well water that makes them so good.

BRINED DILL PICKLES

30 small pickling cucumbers
½ cup coarse salt
2 quarts well water
2 tablespoons vinegar
6 cloves garlic
1 teaspoon pickling spice
½ teaspoon mustard seed
10 sprigs fresh dillweed

Boil the water and cool it. Wash the cucumbers. Layer the cucumbers and dillweed in a gallon-sized stoneware crock. Add all the other ingredients to the water and pour over the cucumbers, making sure the liquid covers the cucumbers. Weight down the cucumbers with a heavy plate. Loosely cover the crock with cheesecloth. Put in a cool place for 5 days to a week. Start testing the pickles toward the end of the week. A pickle at this stage is known to pickle fanatics as half done. Mature pickles are, of course, more sour. When the pickles are ready, put them into the icebox. A note about scum: When it forms, pull it away with a paper towel. It's not poisonous.

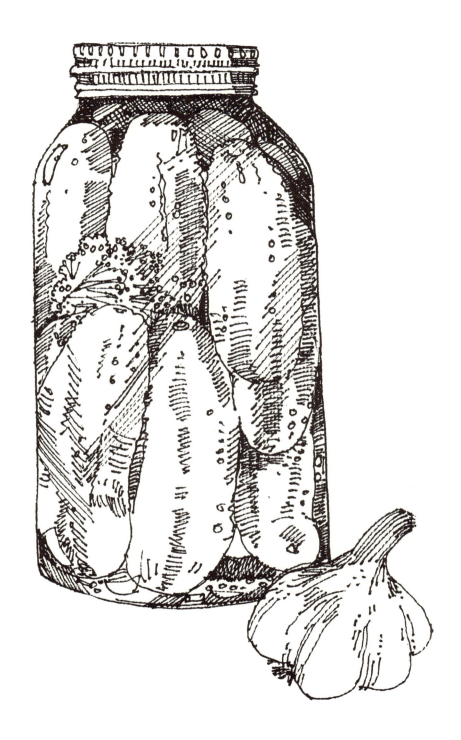

Try to tell a New Englander that Wisconsin might have anything as beautiful as New England in the way of landscape, shoreline, boats, or buildings. You'll get an argument.

I finally persuaded a "down easter" Maine friend to visit. She was astounded. After a tour of the county's highlights, her next to the last gasp of New England chauvinism went like this: "Well, you don't have our salt marshes."

So we don't.

And as she stopped to photograph the lovely board-and-batten church in Fish Creek, she said, "Our churches are older."

Indeed, a good many of them are. But ours have the same purity of line. They are, as the French would put it, worth a detour, whether for worship, a souvenir snapshot, or an evening church supper.

The way I figure it, a church supper is the one way a stranger can get some true home cooking up here. A lucky eater might get to sample any of the following.

SALMON PIE

single crust baked for 3
    minutes
2 cups salmon, fresh or
    canned
2 dozen crumbled saltine
    crackers
2 small eggs, beaten
1 teaspoon salt (scant)
½ teaspoon pepper
pinch cayenne
light cream or buttermilk

Preheat the oven to 350 degrees. Toss all the ingredients together except for the cream. Put the filling into the pie shell. Pour a little cream over the top, taking care not to overflow the shell. Put in the oven and bake 40 minutes. Serve warm. The plain fact is fresh salmon makes a more delectable pie.

SWEDISH POTATO SALAD

6 cold boiled potatoes
4 pickled beets
1 small cucumber
1 dill pickle
1 apple
1 tablespoon capers

Dressing:
½ cup oil-and-vinegar
    dressing
1 generous teaspoon sugar
1 teaspoon grated
    horseradish

Peel the potatoes and cut into thin strips. Cube the beets. Chop the cucumber, pickle, and apple. Arrange the vegetables in layers. Pour the dressing over all. Marinate several hours in the icebox. Just before serving, drain off the dressing and pour again over the top of the salad.

SMOKED SALMON TIDBITS

½ pound boned smoked
    salmon
1 small package creamed
    cheese
1 generous tablespoon sour
    cream
dash Tabasco sauce
salt and pepper
1 tablespoon chopped
    dillweed

Grind or chop the salmon very fine. Mash the cheese and mix thoroughly into the salmon. Add the sour cream and a dash of Tabasco. Salt and pepper very lightly. Chill several hours. Just before serving, form into patties and dredge in the dillweed. Put on a platter and garnish liberally with celery sticks, small pickles, and quartered tomatoes.

A cook can make a lifelong reputation on one superb batch of rosettes. The art of making them can best be learned at a grandmother's knee. If there are no available grandmothers, an enterprising cook might want to devote several batches towards learning on his or her own.

ROSETTES

¾ cup flour, sifted
1 teaspoon salt (scant)
2 teaspoons sugar
1 egg, beaten
½ cup milk
fat for deep frying
powdered sugar

Beat the wet ingredients into the dry ones with a good wire balloon whip. Heat the fat for frying. Put in the rosette iron. Remove and drain it briefly. When the fat is good and hot, dip the rosette iron into the batter and then into the hot fat. If the batter does not stick to the iron, it is too thin. Thicken it with a bit more flour and begin again. Hold the battered rosette iron in the hot oil about two minutes, until the rosette is golden. Remove and slip the rosette in a brown paper grocery bag for draining. Using a powder sugar shaker, shake sugar over the rosettes. Serve hot or cold.

Two Scandinavian favorites I've not tried to duplicate in my old kitchen are lutefisk and lefse. Lutefisk is dried lingcod that has been soaked and treated with slaked lime and soda. Lefse is the potato flatbread that is served with it. I'm not Swedish, Danish, or Norwegian, so I don't have to profess to be crazy for lutefisk. Those dying to try it can attend a church supper during Christmas season and eat their fill.

The same Maine friend is a barn aficionado. We both are. I'd been given the barn (and diner) tour in Maine, and a gorgeous one it was, weaving up and down the coastline, careening inland along the rivers. Door County has no real diners, but its barns stand up against any I know in this country, and I could hardly wait to get her on the road.

We made a real production of it, combining working barns with barn galleries, beginning at the Tria, then down to the Ingwersen and Edgewood Orchard. In between we zigzagged back roads, stopping at each old beauty to sketch a little and eat alot. For this was a progressive tour and picnic. I can't imagine a more fulfilling long summer's day.

Progressive Barn Tour Picnic

cold borscht
salmon seviche
curried chicken salad
bread and butter
fresh currant dessert

QUICK COLD BORSCHT

1 medium can beets
1 medium can tomatoes
1 small onion, finely chopped
lump of butter
1 teaspoon fresh lemon juice
handful chopped parsley
½ teaspoon salt
½ teaspoon sugar

Cube the beets, saving all the juice. Put the tomatoes in the blender and puree. Sauté the onion in butter. Add the beets, juice, tomatoes, lemon juice, salt, and sugar. Bring to a boil and simmer 10 minutes. Add the parsley. Chill until serving time. Put into a wide-mouthed thermos for picnicking. Add a dollop of sour cream to each cup of soup.

SALMON SEVICHE

2 cups fresh salmon, boned and cut into chunks
juice of 1 large lime
2 jalapeño peppers, sliced thin
1 large sweet onion, sliced very fine

Squeeze the lime juice over the salmon. Toss all the ingredients together with a light hand. Marinate in the icebox for at least 12 hours. The lime juice will "cook" the fish. This is a fine treat to serve with cocktails accompanied with a crisp Norwegian hardtack.

CURRIED CHICKEN SALAD

2 cups cooked chicken, cubed
2 cups grapes, sliced in two
¾ cup walnut quarters
2 teaspoons curry powder
1 teaspoon salt
dash cayenne pepper
2 teaspoons lemon juice
1 cup mayonnaise

Simmer or steam a chicken until it is done. Remove the skin. Remove the chicken from the bones and cube it into bite-sized pieces. Combine all the ingredients and chill the salad for several hours.

FRESH CURRANT DESSERT

1 quart red currants
1 quart water
1½ cups sugar
3 tablespoons cornstarch

Wash and drain the currants. Put in a kettle and cover with the water. Add the sugar and bring to boiling. Boil 20 minutes and strain. Return the juice to the heat. Mix the cornstarch with a little cold water and stir into the currant juice. Boil until thick, stirring often. Chill and serve with cream or vanilla custard sauce. 6 servings.

This picnic calls for a bottle or two of chilled white wine. A Johannisberg Riesling is a good choice, as would be a bottle of dry champagne. Remember, however, that Wisconsin's driving and drinking penalties are severe. Unless you plan to hire a teetotaling chauffeur, the choices ought to be a bottle of sparkling grape juice or a thermos of iced tea.

Although I can pump my own gas, I don't wish to learn how to change a tire. No doubt I'll be sorry some day, for I'm told gallantry in truck drivers is on the wane. I also don't care to learn how to make cheese, no matter how easy such slick magazines as *Country Living* assure me the process is. Besides, the state of Wisconsin is full of cheese makers, and deliver me from giving them any homey competition.

The sight of a Lake to Lake cheese label in my Colorado grocery store, with its miniature map of Door County, gives me a severe twinge of homesickness. I immediately buy several packages.

In the county, I'm apt to stop at one of the cheese houses along the highway. Being part Scots, with a houseful of cheese eaters, I buy an armful of whatever is "on special." The bulk of this cheese goes to tacos, pizzas, and toasted cheese sandwiches. When the cook revolts, the family is treated to a dish with slightly more exotic overtones, such as any of the following.

FETTUCCINI WITH BUTTER AND CHEESE

1 pound fettuccini or broad noodles
4 large handfuls freshly grated Parmesan cheese
  or
2 parts cheddar, 1 part Parmesan, 1 part Swiss
¼ pound butter
½ pint whipping cream, slightly whipped
freshly ground pepper

Have the butter at room temperature. Cut it into small pieces and put into a bowl. Add the grated cheese and cream. Cook the noodles *al dente*. Drain them. Heat a large serving bowl and dinner plates. Add the noodles to the serving bowl and begin tossing in handfuls of the cheese, butter, and cream mixture. Toss lightly and keep adding until the sauce is used up. Grind in the black pepper and serve immediately. 6 servings.

The following recipe and any others in the book with a southwestern flavor are presented here to recall the days of the migrant workers in Door County who came up from Mexico and Texas to pick cherries and apples. In migrant housing throughout the peninsula they cooked chilies and beans and made their own tortillas.

GREEN CHILI RELLENOS

6 green chilies
½ pound Wisconsin brick cheese, grated
3 eggs, separated
1 teaspoon water
2 generous teaspoons flour
1 teaspoon salt
peanut oil for frying

Open a can of chilies and lay each one out on a breadboard. Stuff them with cheese. Beat the egg yolks in a small bowl. Beat the egg whites in another bowl. Add the flour, salt, and water to the yolks, beating all the while to assure no lumps. Fold in the egg whites with care. Meanwhile, heat oil in a large, heavy skillet or wok. Using a saucer, slip a chili into the batter and out again. Slip the chili from the saucer into the hot oil. Fry chilies two at a time until golden brown and puffed. Drain and serve immediately. These ought to be the best chili rellenos you've ever eaten. They'll make your reputation as a southwestern cook in Door County. Serve with rice, warm flour tortillas, and a little hot salsa on the side.

For generations, Parisians went down to the central market, Les Halles, for this soup and a jug of red wine after an evening at the theater or a concert. The same supper can easily be put together in Door County after an evening at Peninsula Players, Birch Creek, or the annual music festival.

FRENCH ONION SOUP

2 quarts homemade chicken broth
4 large white onions, sliced
butter
½ pound Wisconsin Swiss cheese
8 slices French bread

Sauté the onions in a good lump of butter until limp. Heat the chicken broth in a large, heavy pot. Add the onions and simmer for an hour. Grate the cheese. Lightly butter the French bread slices and toast in a 350-degree oven about 10 minutes. Float the bread slices in the soup. Sprinkle grated cheese on the top. Transfer the pot to the oven. Raise the heat to 400 degrees. Bake the soup for about 15 minutes, until the cheese is melted and both the bread and cheese are browned on top.

Not too many years ago, there was downhill skiing in the county. The little area with its rope tow was a few miles below Fish Creek at the edge of Highway 42. The mountain attracted skiers from the peninsula and south who hadn't the time or the inclination to drive up to Iron Mountain, Michigan.

Those were the days of long, heavy hickory skis and bear-trap bindings. Ask Bob Lapp, who captains a charter fishing boat in Gills Rock. He has engaging tales to tell about that era, when he and Eddie Valentine and others kept the rope tow running and taught youngsters to ski.

Today, the hotshot downhillers have gone west, and cross-country skiing has become a contender with the snowmobile in the county. Many hotels and motels remain open in winter to bed and feed a new generation of skiers. The Omnibus is a center for the sport. Hundreds of miles of trails are now marked in state parks throughout the county. Trails along the frozen shores are surely the most magnificent.

Ski touring is no time for gourmet food and drink. I once made a day tour with a fellow who pulled off his knapsack at lunch and drew out miniature ham and cheese quiches and splits of vintage wine. The rest of us looked up from our hunks of cheese and sausage. Envy spread around the group. Still, I believe we were on the right track; the less fuss and weight the better for touring. What is wanted is the highest concentration of energy-producing foods at the least weight and the greatest amount of liquid at the least weight. Wine, in the end, is energy sapping, and the weight of the bottle is better replaced by a small plastic jug of water or juice.

The food for lunch on a day tour might include crackers, hard-boiled eggs, and slices of cheese and sausage, the outer peeling of the sausage pared away at home to spare cold fingers. Sandwiches are in order, but don't skimp on fillings. Take along a small thermos of hot soup or spiced tea. A sliced orange is a nice addition and may be shared with other members of the group. And there's gorp, that lovely stuff with the Tolkienesque name.

GORP

Mix equal measures of:
raisins
snipped dried apricots
nuts
sunflower seeds
large chunks of granola

Add a half measure of M&M's or chocolate chips. Pack in plastic bags. I like to keep a small bag of gorp in my jacket pocket, handy for nibbling on the trail.

Another high-protein snack is beefy jerky. Both jerky and pemmican are foods the early settlers borrowed from the Indians. The recipe below has been brought up-to-date.

JERKY

3 pounds lean round steak or venison
1 tablespoon salt
1 tablespoon brown sugar
1 clove garlic, pressed
¾ teaspoon black pepper
⅓ cup soy sauce
⅓ cup Kitchen Bouquet sauce

Freeze the meat, then partially thaw to make it easy to cut into thin strips. Blend all the other ingredients in a large bowl. Put the meat into the marinade overnight. Put the strips on cookie racks fitted over cookie sheets. Bake in a 250-degree oven for half an hour. Lower the oven temperature to 150 degrees and bake another 2 hours until dry.

PEMMICAN

beef suet
dried fruits
dried venison
salt

Combine equal amounts of suet, fruits, and venison. Pound together, adding salt to taste. Form into thin bricks and bake in a 150-degree oven for several hours.

After a day of touring, appetites are keen. It is one of the few times I would wish for a cook in my kitchen. I like to imagine stamping the snow off my boots and walking in the back door, assailed by the rich smell of soup steaming on the stove and the sight of a small and perfect smorgasbord laid out on the old oak table.

The smorgasbord, a Swedish tradition, had its beginnings in what we Americans call potluck, with each guest bringing a dish and the respective cooks outdoing themselves in the elegance of presentation. It would take one formidable expert to manage them all.

Even a scaled-down smorgasbord for after skiing must include one herring dish. The inclusion of soup here, to be eaten before, during, or after the spread, according to the guests' fancy, is not traditional.

ORCHARDS AND FIELDS

Après Ski Smorgasbord
bread and butter
pickled herring
egg with caviar
bird's nest
meatballs
boiled potatoes
green salad
cheeses
chicken soup with barley
glogg
coffee
cookies
beer, aquavit, or schnapps

EGG WITH CAVIAR

3 hard-boiled eggs
1 cup whipping cream
4 tablespoons caviar
2 tablespoons chopped onion
toast points

Whip the cream and fold in the caviar and onions. Place in a mound on a handsome platter. Slice the eggs and arrange around the mound. Make a border with toast slices. Serve right away. 6 servings.

BIRD'S NEST

8 anchovy fillets, chopped
2 tablespoons onion, chopped
2 tablespoons capers
1 tablespoon chives, chopped
2 tablespoons pickled beets, diced
1 cold boiled potato, diced
3 large, raw egg yolks

Arrange the ingredients in alternating rings on a platter. Carefully place the egg yolks on top. Serve right away. The first person to take the dish should mix the ingredients together.

GOOD STRONG COFFEE

coffee
1 egg
water
pinch salt

To make 8 cups of coffee, take a clean, old-fashioned graniteware pot and measure into it 8 tablespoons of coffee that you have mixed with ½ of a beaten egg, a small pinch of salt, and 1 crushed eggshell. Pour over it 8 cups of cold water. Bring slowly to a boil. When the coffee boils, count to ten slowly and remove the pot from the heat. Pour 1 cup of cold water over the coffee to settle the grounds. Wait several minutes and serve.

GLOGG

A cautionary note for skiers who may be bone tired, with muscles like rubber: This drink could put you on the floor. The best medicine for after-ski drinking is several glasses of water, before taking strong spirits.

1 bottle aquavit or brandy
1 bottle dry red wine
12 cardamom seeds
6 cloves
dried peel of 1 orange
1 cup blanched almonds
1 cup seedless raisins
1 cinnamon stick
½ pound lump sugar

Pour the spirits into a large kettle. Add the remaining ingredients except for the sugar. Cover and bring slowly to just below the boiling point. Remove from the heat. Put the sugar on a grill and place over another kettle. Ignite the hot glogg and pour it over the sugar until the sugar melts. Ladle into punch cups with almonds and raisins. Glogg may be cooled and reheated, but take care not to let it boil.

SPRITZ COOKIES

1 cup butter
½ cup sugar
1 egg
2½ cups flour
½ teaspoon vanilla

Cream the butter and sugar until fluffy. Add the egg and vanilla and beat again. Mix in the flour thoroughly. Put through a cookie press and shape into wreaths. Bake in a hot oven at 425 degrees about 8 minutes, until golden.

JOY'S DANISH COOKIES

2 eggs
1 cup sugar
1 teaspoon lemon extract
1 cup lard
3 cups flour
½ teaspoon salt
½ teaspoon soda
½ teaspoon baking powder

Cream the lard and sugar. Add the eggs and lemon extract and beat well. Add the dry ingredients and mix in thoroughly. Chill several hours. Roll out on a well-floured pastry board. Bake at 350 degrees for 8 to 10 minutes, until golden.

·ROOTS·

Roots have become a grand national preoccupation. Those roots that many of us midwesterners fled from in our youth, we're back looking for now. All the Midwest tradition that we used to call provincial—the family reunions, the church suppers, the coin showers in the country taverns—we want to catch hold of one more time.

Door County is layered in tradition, perhaps particularly the southern Door.

Take a back road, any back road, and you're likely to come upon a country tavern at the next crossroad. Chances are the food is good, the drinks are inexpensive, and everything is served in abundance.

I know people in Green Bay who collect and hoard a list of country bars. They argue as to the merits of one Friday fish fry over another, or who has the best chicken on Sundays, and, of course, who serves up the cheapest drinks.

These taverns (called farmer bars when I was young, and no disparagement intended) are generally worth a detour even if you're not hungry. Sometimes you find them in a corner of an old opera house, with an elegant, rococo Victorian back bar. Now the opera house itself might be used for country swing dancing on weekends or even for auctions. Others were built for business on their own, with space enough to take in a wedding, country style and size.

I've been there for the wedding dances. All the food and drink you can manage, a dance with the bride if you pin a dollar bill on her satin gown, and a polka band that plays double-time polkas and schottisches. Everyone dances; it's like the movies, the nostalgia-based films where the eighty-year-old great-grandfather is waltzing with the four-year-old flower girl. But it's real, the hall is hot, and everyone is dripping wet. The bridesmaids are rainbow girls, all the colors swimming across the floor.

You'd better take home a piece of the wedding cake. Put it under your pillow and sleep tight. Still, I'd rather eat kneecaps, one after another, instead of cake. And here is a recipe.

KNEECAPS

2 cakes compressed yeast
¼ cup lukewarm water
¾ cup scalded milk
½ cup shortening
½ cup sugar
¾ teaspoon salt
2 eggs
6 cups flour (approximate)
hot fat for frying

Crumble the yeast into the water. Scald the milk and cool. Cream the shortening, sugar, and salt. Add the eggs and mix again. Add the milk and yeasted water. Add the flour a cup at a time. When the dough blisters on working it, add no more flour. Knead for 8 minutes. Place the dough in a greased bowl, cover, and let rise in a warm place until nearly double. Punch the dough down and roll it on a floured board to a half inch thickness. Cut with a biscuit cutter into circles. Let rise another 30 minutes or until nearly double. Press with your thumb in the center of each. Heat the fat in a deep kettle. When the fat is nearly smoking, fry the kneecaps, 3 at a time, until golden. Drain and dip in powdered sugar. Cool. Fill with jam, blueberry or cherry filling, or whipped cream.

On Friday nights it's fish: smelt in season and otherwise perch, which climbs steadily in price because the catch is short and the waters are polluted.

Smelt, though, are the same bargain they were when I was a child. When they're running, you might find a country tavern that passes a heaped platter of fried smelt down the bar. Grab one quick and eat it with your fingers. Hot. Eat everything, bones and all, unless it's oversized.

SMELTS WISCONSIN BAR STYLE

If you have a deep-fat fryer with a basket, dredge the smelts in flour or fine cornmeal and use your favorite frying recipe. Otherwise, take the easy way out and oven-bake your smelts.

a mess of small smelts
milk
flour
oil
butter

Clean the smelts, wash, and dry thoroughly. Dip them in milk, shake dry, and dredge in flour. Take a large, flat baking pan and cover the bottom with a small amount of vegetable oil or a mix of oil and butter. Lay the smelts in the pan and put it in a 450-degree oven. Bake for a few minutes; flip the smelts over and continue to bake, perhaps a total of 7 or 8 minutes. Remove to a hot platter and serve with tartar sauce or lemon juice.

Standard fare at most country bars is a jar of pickled pigs' feet or a jar of pickled eggs. I'd try a pickled smelt myself, if I were offered one.

PICKLED SMELTS

4 cups water
2½ cups vinegar
4 teaspoons sugar
4 teaspoons salt
12 whole cloves
12 whole peppercorns
3 bay leaves
1 large onion, halved

Put all the above ingredients in a large, heavy kettle with an enameled interior. Bring to a boil. Turn to simmer and let the ingredients get acquainted for about a half hour. Slip in a small mess of smelt, perhaps a dozen or so, that have been cleaned. Do not boil. Heat through, then allow to cool. Store in the icebox. This same recipe can be used to pickle any fish you might catch or buy in Door County, with delicious results.

I'm not sure how quick I'd be to try the next delectable. Among the squeamish memories of childhood was learning to swim in leech-infested waters. Wading out, watching my father's eyes on me, struggling to learn the crawl when I knew that afterwards I'd run to shore with my legs covered with suckers. Even two or three were enough to set my teeth chattering.

In all my years of Door County swimming, I've never encountered one leech and therefore concluded there are none in the county. Still, the following recipe came to me from a native of the southern part of the county who swears there are plenty of suckers around these parts if only I cared to go looking.

This recipe appears as I received it.

PICKLED SUCKERS OF DISPUTED ORIGIN

Take a bunch of suckers. Easy to catch them—just go swimming. Pry them off and throw them in a bucket. Then go home and make a pickling juice. [See the recipe for pickled smelt for ingredients and directions.] Clean those suckers. If they're big, cut in pieces. Salt them like when you want to fry them. Let them stand overnight. Wipe them dry. Cook them in the pickle juice, real gentle, and don't let them boil up or they'll be too tough to eat.
Note: And refrigerate afterwards, please.

On Saturday nights, there are generally country bands and family-style chicken dinners. Sometimes, tucked between the mashed potatoes and gravy boats there's a platter of frog legs. I tell myself I know where they came from: Frog Station, just out of the county on County Trunk K in Kewaunee County. The peeper chorus there would raise the dead.

I haven't caught a frog since I was a kid in Mr. Hubbard's biology class at East High, Green Bay. (Hub's Motel, Sister Bay, was his summer work establishment.) We caught frogs, we dissected them. If you go out frogging, all you want are the legs. Skin them as you would peel off a glove, and chill before cooking.

FROG LEGS WITH GARLIC

18 large frog legs
milk
seasoned flour
vegetable oil
butter
3 cloves garlic, finely chopped
lemon juice
fresh parsley, chopped

Dip the legs in milk and dredge in seasoned flour. Heat the oil in a large, heavy skillet, enough to cover the bottom of the pan about a quarter of an inch. When the oil is just below the smoking point, lay in the frog legs gently and cook quickly on all sides. This should take about 8 or 9 minutes. Remove them to a hot platter. Drain off most of the oil and add a good knob of butter. Brown the butter; add the garlic. Cook a minute, but take care not to let the garlic burn. Remove from the heat and add the juice of half a lemon. Mix quickly and pour over the frog legs. Sprinkle with parsley and serve immediately. Serves 6.

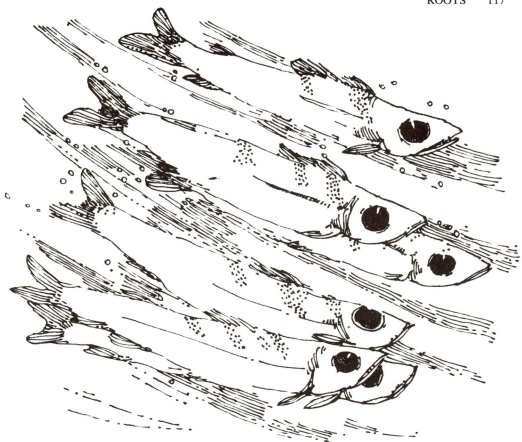

If catching peepers is not your idea of an evening's good time, you might prefer to go smelting instead. This Door County sport is enjoyed by natives and goes largely unnoticed by tourists. Spring is the time the smelts start running.

Here's the procedure: Find a native who's willing to divulge a favorite smelt run. Get a good supply of beer, firewood, blankets, a couple of seining nets, and several working flashlights. Don't forget a pair of hip waders, for the water's cold, dark, and very wet, especially at one in the morning.

It's a party. Some of us build up the fire and play cards to pass the time. We sing camp and school songs until we've run through them all at least twice and finally lost our common voice. Then, after building up the fire for the tenth time, someone shouts, "They're running!"

The dead come to life and we're out there seining. We get our mess of smelts. We think we're going to cook them by the side of the stream. But we don't. We load up our paraphernalia and plan a feast for the evening after.

Pass through Brussels on your way north on Highway 57 and you're in the middle of little Belgium. The Red Owl store at the outskirts carries such specialties as kolaches, Belgian prune pies, and Belgian tripe (pronounced *trip*). For those

who would be warded off, this is a harmless variation on the bratwurst, a combination of sausage meat and kraut. It was probably invented by a farmer who was long on cabbage and short on hogs. In any case, it's worth trying, and there are plenty of devotees around who've become addicted. I cook tripe as I do brats, but minus the beer and onions, for they've already a decided life of their own.

BRUSSELS'S BELGIAN TRIPE

12 tripes
water or broth

Simmer the tripes in water or any handy homemade broth until they are just cooked through. Grease a heavy skillet and continue to cook until done or transfer them to a hot charcoal fire and finish cooking that way. Serve as you would brats, with plenty of mustard, pickles, and potato salad or boiled, buttered potatoes. 6 servings.

A real treat in summer is a Belgian *kirmiss*—a Catholic Mass plus a worldly celebration, where you can get all the treats mentioned above as well as beer, music, and chicken booyah. The word *booyah* itself gives off a certain effervescence and seems to call for festivity. It is, in fact, a glorified chicken stew, one of those dishes that benefits from being made in great quantity in an iron caldron. By rights it should be a winter's meal, for it is one that warms the bones. But don't miss the chance to taste it in summer at a church picnic or at Brussels's famous Belgian days.

CHICKEN BOOYAH VAN BELLINGER

1 pound stewing beef, cubed small
2 stewing hens
2½ pounds potatoes
1 bunch celery
1 green pepper
1½ pounds onions
1 small head cabbage
1 can corn
1 pound green beans
1 fistful carrots
1 box frozen green peas
salt and pepper
fresh parsley (optional)

Boil the beef in several quarts of water. While the beef is cooking, take the plump hens and cut them in pieces. Add to the cooking pot. Chop all the vegetables. Sauté the onions in a bit of butter or chicken fat. Add the pepper, celery, cabbage, and carrots when the chicken is beginning to get tender. Cook perhaps 20 minutes longer and add the potatoes and green beans. When the chicken is tender, remove it with a slotted spoon and take the meat from the bones. Put back into the pot and add the corn and peas. Salt and pepper to taste. Allow to cool and reheat just before serving. A fistful of finely chopped parsley is not "kosher" but will give the booyah a subtle flavor. Add a bit of water if the stew seems too thick. Serve the booyah with a crusty loaf or the traditional hard rolls called semmels. A summer greens salad is a fine accompaniment. This recipe makes about 4 gallons and will serve a crowd.

Dessert by rights should be Belgian pie. "What is a Belgian pie," a couple asked me the other day. "Is it one of those jokes they tell around here?" After assuring them it was *not* one of those jokes and that the pie could be found at the Brussels Red Owl, the woman insisted she wanted to eat it sitting down. A *kirmiss*, I told her, you'll have to find a *kirmiss* on your way back to Chicago.

BELGIAN PIE

This recipe makes 5 small pies and should suffice for a booyah crowd.

4 tablespoons sugar
4 tablespoons shortening
1 egg, beaten
½ teaspoon salt
4 teaspoons baking powder
1 cup milk
flour

Cream the shortening and sugar. Add the egg and the milk. Mix the baking powder and salt with the first cup of flour. Mix this in and keep adding flour slowly until you have a soft dough. Let the dough rest 10 minutes. Flour a board and roll out 5 rounds of pie crust.

Filling:
1 package prunes, pitted and cooked
1 pound cottage cheese
½ cup cream
¾ cup sugar
2 eggs, beaten
pinch salt
pinch nutmeg

Brush each pie crust with beaten egg white. Pop in a 425-degree oven for 2 minutes. Remove. Drain any extra moisture from the prunes to prevent sogginess. Put prunes in each crust. Mix the other ingredients and put them through a sieve or blend on the fine blade of a food processor. Distribute on each pie. Bake at 425 degrees for 20 to 25 minutes. Cool and serve.

Among other church activities I look out for are bazaars, preferably those that sell food on the premises or have a handy tavern next door that does. These bazaars turn out to be centers for contemporary folk art, and you may find a wood chopper whirligig, any number of bird and beast yard ornaments, even matchstick and Popsicle-stick art, along with all the knitted mittens, doilies, and potholders.

The white elephant section is not to be missed. I once took home a glass necklace for a quarter that turned out to be hand-cut Bohemian crystal. In any case, I've furnished a kitchen from these sales and wouldn't give up any of the old knives, choppers, sieves, wooden spoons, and iron pots for new ones. A *batterie de cuisine* for under twenty dollars is certainly a pecuniary cook's dream.

Among the shining jars of jelly and corn relishes, I've found more earnest and sturdy country delicacies. Take, for example, pickled pigs' feet and headcheese. Both are excellent with a good Wisconsin beer such as Augsburger or

Leinenkugel and a loaf of dark, heavy rye, the two-pound, dense variety, which, sadly, cannot be found in Door County.

COOKING PIGS' FEET

pigs' feet
water
salt
allspice
garlic
peppercorns

Clean and scrape the pigs' feet well. Scald in hot water and scrape again. Place in a kettle, cover with cold water, and bring to a boil. Skim off the froth and add the seasonings. For 8 pigs' feet, use several quarts of water, 2 tablespoons salt, and a small handful of peppercorns and allspice. Drop in several split cloves of garlic while the feet are cooking. Simmer at least three hours. Test for tenderness with a small, sharp knife. Cool the feet in a bowl; strain some of the stock and pour it over them. Serve them with a strong mustard, pickles, and a dish of lentils. Or, pickle them.

PICKLED PIGS' FEET

2 cups vinegar
2 cups water
1 teaspoon salt
½ teaspoon sugar
1 generous tablespoon pickling spices
6 peppercorns

Heat the vinegar, water, salt, and sugar to just below the boiling point. Mix in the pickling spices and peppercorns. Put the pigs' feet in a glass baking dish. Pour the marinade over them. Leave them a day in a cool place, turning them occasionally in the marinade. Store in the refrigerator.

HEADCHEESE

A word of explanation before beginning. This recipe is a labor of love and not for those with squeamish, city stomachs. In hog butchering nothing is wasted, not even the head. Hence this delicacy. You may, however, substitute pork shoulder for a hog's head; the result is very close, though not as flavorful.

1 hog's head, cleaned and soaked in water 8 hours
2 pounds lean pork
1 piece pork rind
    or
8 to 10 pounds pork shoulder
1 piece pork rind

First seasonings:
2 cloves
1½ tablespoon salt
6 peppercorns
1 bay leaf
1 small onion, sliced
1 carrot, sliced

Second seasonings:
2 tablespoons salt
2 teaspoons white pepper
½ teaspoon allspice
1/8 teaspoon ground cloves

Put the meat in a heavy kettle and cover with cold water. Add the first group of seasonings. Bring to a boil and skim away the foam. Simmer the meat until tender, approximately 2½ hours. Drain the meat, reserving the stock. Slice into thin pieces. Put an old, clean dish towel in a deep, large bowl, draping the edges over the sides. Line with the rind. Arrange the meat and fat in alternate layers, sprinkling a mixture of the second group of seasonings over them. Cover the meat with the rind. Pull together the dish towel tightly and tie with a string. Put this bundle back into the kettle, cover with reserved stock, and cook 15 minutes. Remove the bundle to a large platter. Cover with a large bread board. Lay several heavy stones, bricks, or other weights on top. Leave the headcheese under the weights for at least 24 hours. Slice thin and serve with a hearty mustard or horseradish sauce. Store in the refrigerator. 30 servings.

I'm crazy for parades. I'd run a mile to catch a drum-and-bugle corps swinging around a corner. Whatever cadence they're playing. I'm marching inside. Door County in season is a feast of parades. The Olde Ellison Bay Days parade is our

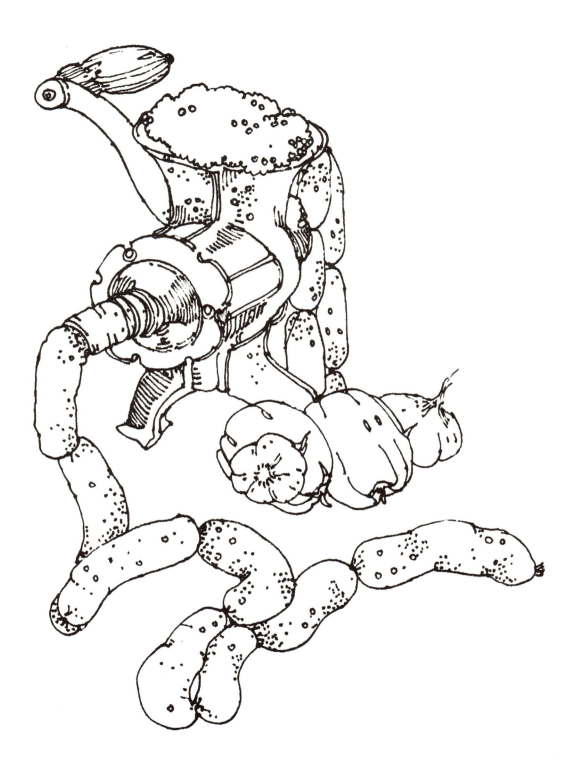

favorite, *that* weekend; but come the Fourth of July, we debate over the merits of Egg Harbor's versus Baileys Harbor's.

One Fourth we made them all: the steam engine properly terrified everyone; Uncle Sam on his stilts walked right over the head of my seven-year-old; the Thumb Fun Haunted House inhabitants were surely the spookiest they'd ever been; and the bands set us marching in step.

The children scrambled for penny candy from every float, and despite the fact that their stomachs were full by lunchtime, we forced them to eat a bratwurst with the rest of us. The brats in Egg Harbor were not the same as those in Baileys Harbor because, of course, they'd been made by different butchers. Brat fans are legion in Wisconsin, and the hard-core are devoted to certain butchers. Wurst recipes, refined over the years, are trade secrets, sometimes as strictly guarded as IBM research materials.

I've not been an industrial spy in the back room of my favorite brat maker, but I do have a recipe that will match almost any sausage around. This recipe makes patties. If you want a regular wurst, search out a sausage stuffer at a county antique story, pry some casings loose from a meat-packer, and you're in business.

FOURTH OF JULY BRATWURST

1 tablespoon salt
1 tablespoon MSG
1 cup finely chopped parsley (optional)
1 teaspoon marjoram
1 teaspoon thyme
⅓ cup sage (scant)
1 tablespoon black pepper
5 pounds pork fillet, finely ground
1 pound rindless pork fat, finely ground
2 bunches scallions, finely chopped (optional)

Take a large bowl, put in all the ingredients, and work them together with your hands. You might want to test the sausage for taste by frying bits in a small pan. When it suits your taste, push the ingredients through the stuffer into links. Separate into packages and cook or freeze. This amount of sausage should serve 16 easily.

Home from the parades that Fourth of July, we waited for the regatta and fireworks in the harbor at Gills Rock. Rumor had it that the President had been invited but might be sending an upper mucky-muck of the admiralty in his stead.

The sky was clear, with a strong blow coming in from the northwest. This scotched the entry of any but large sailboats in the regatta. We gave all boats special marks for braving choppy seas and cheered the fishing tugs especially, for they took the big waves broadside.

At sunset, we settled in on the stone beach to watch the fireworks, with blankets, sparklers, and a bucketful of home-fried chicken.

With the last of the display, Nature herself took over, and we were treated to the northern lights. We sat amazed for another long hour, watching the great pulses of light shifting and streaking over our heads. There wasn't a sound up and down Hedgehog Harbor, though we could see dots of fires along its rim.

The next day, while eating the leftover chicken, we agreed there'd not been another Fourth like it. And here, as an addendum, is how I fix that chicken. A real Wisconsin farm bird is what I look for, not one of those cold-storage types from Arkansas.

EMILY'S DOWN-HOME FRIED CHICKEN

This recipe arrived in Door County by way of Virginia. It was learned at the knee of a black cook of superb reputation. It is one of those seemingly simple recipes that may take several doings to reach the desired effect. A heavy iron skillet of generous proportions and a tight fitting lid are essential.

2 frying chickens
cooking oil
flour
salt and pepper

Cut up the chickens and wash. Drain in a colander. Put a generous amount of flour into a paper bag. Add a healthy pinch of salt and a small handful of ground pepper. Shake the chicken pieces in the flour. Meanwhile, have at least an inch of oil heating inthe skillet. When the oil has reached the smoking point, put in the breasts. Immediately put the lid on the skillet. The fat, as Emily says, should surprise the food, and this is what accounts for that sweet succulence in the finished product. Fry a few minutes, then turn the breasts skin side up. When done, the chicken will be brown and crusty but not burnt. Remove the breasts to a heated platter. Reheat the oil and fry the dark meat in a similar fashion. Serve immediately. 8 generous servings.

Among the notable traffic stoppers of the summer is the Red Barn's tailgate antique sale. This feast of the good old stuff and more recent collectibles is held annually on July 27th, coinciding with the house-and-garden walk. Literally thousands of cars crawl back and forth past the Red Barn complex, stopping to look and buy. Dealers from around the Midwest arrive in the small hours of the morning to set up their booths and to pray for good weather.

At first glance, I want everything in sight. I'll take the electric blue milk-painted cupboard from one booth and the spatterware jug from another to put in it. I'd like a few old apple baskets and a goose decoy, perhaps a string of early sleigh bells to take home for Christmas.

The latest rage in collectibles is the grapevine wreath. I saw them first at Jack and Mary Kugler's booth at the tailgate sale. These wreaths will go the year around, depending on what you decorate them with, and they are child's play to make.

Door County abounds in wild grapevines. They grow in profusion along the roadsides, and if you don't trim them, the county road crews certainly will. Here's how to add a handsome decoration to your door or mantlepiece.

WILD GRAPEVINE WREATH

Cut at least 18 lengths of vine, about 1 yard long. Pull off the leaves, taking care to leave the tendrils intact. Twist one length to the size wreath you want. Continue weaving the vines into the basic structure. Decorate later with bittersweet, which you can find, if you're lucky, at an autumn farmers' market. Or buy a smattering of silk flowers at Al Johnson's Swedish Butik and weave these in. A real velvet ribbon is a handsome touch for fall and winter. Antique taffeta plaid hair ribbon makes another fine trim.

Note: If you wait until fall to make your wreaths, you may need to soften the vines by soaking them in the bathtub. Avoid the mess and make them in the summer.

If you're starving that day, you'll be hard put to find a Bayside restaurant that isn't mobbed, with a waiting list. You might want to pack a picnic and sit down on your own auto tailgate to rest tired feet. A large thermos of icy spiced tea, a large bunch of grapes, and a stuffed bread makes a simple and delectable shopper's lunch.

TAILGATE PICNIC BREAD

1 loaf French bread
butter
sliced ham
Dijon mustard
bag of alfalfa sprouts

Slit the bread lengthwise and pull off some of the inside of the loaf from each section. Butter both sides. Slip in generous amounts of ham and spread with mustard. Put the bread back together and wrap with waxed paper to preserve the crust. Add the alfalfa sprouts at the last minute.

Another more elegant version of this bread might be taken to your favorite Door County beach after feet and eyes have had their fill of both antiques and houses. Make this a picnic in the French fashion, with stemmed glasses for the wine (even if they come from K-Mart), a small luncheon cloth, and an antique picnic basket. These baskets date from the first decade of the century, are shaped like suitcases, and made of wicker, with clever fastenings both inside and out.

ANOTHER WAY TO STUFF A BREAD

1 long loaf French bread
1 small pot whitefish caviar
1 pound cream cheese
½ pound butter
dash Tabasco sauce
large handful chopped parsley

Proceed as above with the bread. Cream the butter and cheese. Add Tabasco and chopped parsley. Cream again. Spread this mixture into cavities on either side of the loaf. Spread the caviar on the cheese. Fit the bread back together. Slice diagonally into portions.

Among all the general stores I've known, the Pioneer Market in Ellison Bay is my hands-down favorite. I once wrote an article on this store for a Colorado paper, and a young millionaire with plenty of discretionary money to invest called me up and asked how he could pull off such a store in Boulder, Colorado. I told him to forget it, he couldn't. The weight of the past was against him.

There are layers of life in the Pioneer that make a continuum between past and present. At first glance, the store presents the look of a fabulous grandmother's attic. The Newmans must deal year after year with innocents who are determined to buy the antiques.

The antiques stay. They live among the groceries and general merchandise. Some are in daily use: the scales, the big pot-bellied stove, the stool at the front counter once used for customers lingering over the lengths of calico and cambric.

Orderly types long to reorganize the place. But it is in order, an amazing and complicated one. I admit, however, I'd hate to be presented with the task of taking inventory.

The Pioneer is a rescue haven for those in need. Sailors can get ice; anyone can drop off dry cleaning and pick up a library book; a boater who's fallen into the drink can outfit himself with a suit of clothes from the ground up. Then there's all the rest of it: fine Swiss chocolate, English water biscuits, Scandinavian ginger cookies, wild asparagus in season, local maple syrup and honey, books by Door County writers, stamps and cards for desperate lovers, plus any culinary staple a kitchen might need. Excepting fresh fish. For the catch of the day, you need go north to Gills Rock, where the Weborgs can supply whitefish smacking fresh from the water.

When new potatoes start coming in, I buy a peck, and we eat them boiled and drizzled with melted butter and chopped parsley. Getting bored with them, finally, I might fix:

GERMAN FRIED POTATOES

6 strips bacon
12 new potatoes
1 large onion, sliced
1 generous teaspoon caraway seeds
salt and pepper to taste

Fry the bacon in a large, heavy skillet. Remove the bacon and leave the grease in the pan. Slice the potatoes and onion. Heat the grease until hot but not quite smoking. Layer in the potatoes and onions, adding salt and pepper as you do so. Sprinkle caraway seeds on the top. Cook over medium heat for several minutes, then begin to lift and turn the potatoes so that the caraway seeds are mixed in and the bacon grease coats each slice of potato lightly. Continue to cook for about 20 minutes. The potatoes should be golden but not dark brown. Crumble bacon on top and serve from the skillet. 6 servings.

For a company dinner when I have unexpected guests, I sometimes serve a poached fish, a green salad, and what I call a clincher:

BAKED NEW POTATOES

3 new potatoes per person
1 jar fish roe
½ cup melted butter
1 cup sour cream
handful chopped parsley
handful chopped green scallions

Scrub the potatoes lightly, poke a slit into each one with a sharp knife, wipe them with oil, and bake until done. Arrange condiments on a platter, then crosshatch each potato and press open. Add the butter, caviar, sour cream, and a good sprinkle of parsley and scallions. Serve immediately.

In the later part of August, when the apples start to drop from our eighty-year-old apple trees, I cut out the worms and make sauce. Then the family wants potato pancakes. I make them as similar as I can to the article that Kaap's Restaurant in Green Bay used to produce when I was growing up. That marvelous old establishment, with its marble-topped tables and dark booths (where many a romance or business proposition had been born or put to death), is now demolished to make way for yet another mall.

This is a good way to make use of potatoes that are past their prime but *not* moldy.

POTATO PANCAKES JUST LIKE KAAP'S

4 or 5 largish potatoes
or
enough to make 2 cups grated
2 large eggs, beaten
1½ tablespoons flour
1 generous teaspoon salt
good pinch pepper
melted shortening

Peel, then grate the potatoes. Squeeze them in a clean dish towel until all the moisture is gone. This is the imperative trick in making crisp pancakes. Add the eggs to the grated potatoes. Mix in the flour, salt, and pepper. Mix well. Fry the pancakes either on a well-greased griddle or in a heavy frying pan with about ¼ inch of very hot melted shortening. I test the oil by flicking in a drop of water; if it sets up a terrific sizzle and crackle I know it's ready. The pancakes cook in a matter of minutes. Eat them right away or they'll get soggy. If we're out of applesauce, we use Gust Klenke's Door County honey. 4 generous servings.

When my mother was growing up in Marinette in the early part of the century, it was fashionable to take an excursion boat down to Green Bay and dance by moonlight at the Bay Beach Pavilion. The Pavilion still stands, and when I was in high school dances were still being held. The excursion boats, however, were long gone.

Another favorite trip by excursion boat in my mother's salad days was to Ephraim. The point was to take the air, to view the bluffs, and to examine firsthand a picturesque and isolated place which was only beginning to join its own century.

These trips were, and still would be, a most civilized way to travel from one port to another. In my mother's day, it was the *only* civilized way to get to Door County. Land travel was a real test of endurance; the few automobiles that came north found the going rough on mucky, rutted dirt roads. Horses were sure footed in these conditions, of course, and the stage coach ran up to Baileys Harbor as late as 1916.

In his 92nd year, John Ellstrom told me of yet another excursion, how as a teenager he drove cows from Gills Rock down to Green Bay. On foot, and sleeping out at night. You could wear out a pair of boots in one trip down and back.

Slowly, though, the first tourists to the Door began to filter in from Chicago. At first, the visitors stayed in private homes, paying for bed and board, much

the same as American travelers do today in remote corners of Ireland, Scotland, or Wales. These homes soon expanded, adding a room or two and taking visitors in real earnest.

The boarding houses gradually gave way to hotels. A very few were log structures like the Du Nord in Sister Bay. In the main they were great white clapboard piles, built with local lumber. The use of wood in these structures is so lavish by today's standards that it takes one's breath away.

The White Gull and the Thorp in Fish Creek; the Griffin in Ellison Bay; the Liberty Park in Sister Bay; the Edgewater, the Hotel Ephraim, the Evergreen, the Eagle Inn, and the Anderson, all in Ephraim, were the fashionable places to take lodgings. In most cases, they faced to the water, to one harbor or another, and lawn chairs were set out in orderly profusion for taking the air and the view.

Many had gazebos, most had docks and paddle boats and painted rowboats. Lawn games were in great favor. Croquet, shuffleboard, and horseshoes brought out the refined beast in every player. Tennis courts were the ultimate refinement, but pools were unheard of. Golf courses soon followed.

I see, in my mind's eye, the creamy linen suits, the knickers, the filmy summer-afternoon dresses, the sturdy walking shoes that tramped in and out. And the great dinner bell that called guests in to eat at a common table.

Today, one by one, many of these old landmarks are making way for condominiums.

The Anderson Hotel is a perfect case in point. It was founded by Matilda Valentine, the widow of a lumber-schooner captain, who had stopped at Eagle Harbor in Ephraim many times aboard her husband's ship. She'd been an official member of his crew—ship's cook. Of all the Lake Michigan lumber ports, it was Ephraim that took her heart.

Mrs. Valentine opened the Stone Wall Cottage in 1899. I never knew her, of course, but I have her in my head as one of those plucky, talented women who defied Victorian convention by opening her own business. By the standards of the times, she should have put on widow's weeds and gone into seclusion instead.

Business thrived, and several years later the Stone Wall became the Anderson Hotel when she married Adolph Anderson, owner of the village store and the Anderson Dock. Landmarks, all of them, and beloved and photographed by generations of Ephraim residents and visitors.

The hotel was later purchased and operated by Matilda's son, Everett Valentine, and finally by his widow, Kitty, and her son Edward. Throughout its long life, it was famous for its kitchen. The last time I looked, the hotel was being dismantled for another set of condominiums.

Looking back to the old days, I have friends who were lucky enough to raid the kitchen. Here are recipes for some of the treats they managed to scavenge away.

ANDERSON HOTEL STEAMED CHERRY PUDDING

2 cups drained and pitted cherries
¼ cup sugar
¼ cup molasses
¼ teaspoon salt
1½ cups flour
2 teaspoons soda dissolved in ⅓ cup hot water

Take a large bowl and combine the dry ingredients. Add the rest. Combine well. Have at hand a buttered mold or a large juice can. Pour the pudding into the mold, making certain it is no more than ⅔ full. Put a double thickness of waxed paper over the top and tie securely with string. Place the pudding on a rack in a steamer or kettle that has at least an inch of water boiling briskly. Steam the pudding for 1½ to 2 hours. When the pudding is done, remove the waxed paper and allow the pudding to cool before attempting to remove it from the mold.

Sauce:
½ pound butter
2 cups sugar
1 cup cream

Cream the butter (margarine will not do) with the sugar in the top of a double boiler. Add the cream very slowly, mixing well, and remove from the fire when the sauce is heated through. Pour the sauce over each slice of pudding. Should serve 10, but 6 devotees can polish this dessert off with ease.

ANDERSON HOTEL FRESH PEACH PIE

Crust:
1½ cups graham cracker crumbs
⅓ cup butter
⅓ cup brown sugar

Mix all the ingredients and press into a 9-inch pie pan. Bake at 375 degrees for 4 minutes.

Filling:
2 cups powdered sugar
½ cup butter
2 egg yolks
2 egg whites, beaten stiff
4 large or 6 medium peaches, peeled and sliced
½ pint cream, whipped

Cream together the powdered sugar and butter. Stir in the egg yolks, thoroughly. Fold in the egg whites. Pour this mixture into the crust. Add the sliced peaches and cover with the whipped cream. Chill for at least 6 hours.

ANDERSON HOTEL STRAWBERRY PIE

9 inch pie crust, baked
2 quarts Door County strawberries
½ cup sugar
3 tablespoons cornstarch
1 cup water
½ teaspoon salt
½ pint whipped cream

Fill the crust to level with halved, clean strawberries. Mash 1½ cup berries in a heavy-bottomed sauce pan. Add the sugar, cornstarch, water, and salt. Cook over low heat, stirring constantly until the mixture thickens. Pour this mixture over the berries in the crust. Chill for 4 hours and top with whipped cream. Phony whipped cream will not do.

To give proper credit, Door County cookery, whether it be German, Belgian, or Scandinavian, has its underpinnings in housewives' kitchens of the nineteenth century. Just as a painted dower chest or a woven coverlet might be passed to a bride on her wedding day, a compendium of family recipes was often given as well.

These treasures were generally small, bound journals, written by hand. They included "receipts" for making soap, lard, and candles as well as the dishes which hopefully would prove out the old adage: The way to a man's heart is through his stomach.

I've search county estate sales and antique shops for one of the old journals. But in vain. These compendiums of common sense and good cooking generally have been used to death or passed down mother to daughter, mother to daughter.

I've been lucky enough to examine several of these journals and include here several nineteenth century "receipts," adapted for the modern kitchen.

MORAVIAN SUGAR CAKE

This is not a cake as we understand it, but more a raised sweet bread. It has roots in Pennsylvania, arriving in Ephraim with the Moravians in the 1860s, and is still made today in a few Ephraim kitchens.

2 packets yeast
½ cup lukewarm water
1 pint milk, scalded
1 cup mashed potatoes
1 teaspoon salt
5½ to 6 cups flour
2 eggs, beaten
1 cup sugar
½ cup butter
½ cup lard or Crisco
butter
brown sugar
cinnamon

Scald the milk and cool to lukewarm. (Scalding is simply bringing milk just to the boiling point and removing from the heat.) Dissolve the yeast in warm water. Add the milk, mashed potatoes, and salt. Gradually beat in the flour, cup by cup. Beat this mixture well. Cover with a damp, clean cloth and put in a warm place to rise. When the dough has nearly doubled, add the eggs, sugar, and butter or shortening. Add enough flour to make the dough easy to knead. Do this bit by bit, lest you find yourself with a stiff dough that won't be worked. Knead the dough about 10 minutes, until it blisters as you work it. Cover and put the dough aside again to rise. When the dough has nearly doubled, punch it down. Place the dough in shallow, greased cake pans, patting it smooth. Put it aside to rise again. Towards the end of the rising time, very gently punch holes with your thumb at 2-inch intervals across the surface of the cakes. Fill these with a mixture of creamed butter and brown sugar. Dust the tops of the cakes with cinnamon. Bake in a 350-degree oven on the middle rack for about 25 minutes. Take care that the pans don't touch one another. Remove and cool.

MORAVIAN CHRISTMAS COOKIES

½ cup butter
1 cup molasses
1 teaspoon ginger (scant)
1 teaspoon ground gloves (scant)
pinch nutmeg
pinch allspice
pinch salt
¾ teaspoon baking soda
2⅔ cups sifted unbleached flour

Melt the butter, heat the molasses slightly, and mix the two together. Add the spices. Work in the flour, salt, and soda a half cup at a time. Cover the mixture and store in a cool place for at least 2 weeks. This allows the spices to ripen and get properly acquainted. Roll out the dough on a lightly floured board. It should be paper thin. Cut with very small cookie cutters into stars, pine trees, and bells. Bake on a greased cookie sheet for 5 to 6 minutes at 375 degrees. Store in a well-sealed tin. These cookies are well worth the effort. Your friends will ask for the recipe. Particularly nice with afternoon tea or coffee.

VIVIAN'S PEA SOUP

1½ cups dried whole peas
ham bone
salt pork
water
1 cup chopped celery
1 cup chopped carrots
1 cup diced potatoes
2 onions, chopped fine

Soak the peas overnight. Drain in the morning and put to cook in a large kettle, covering with water. In a separate kettle cook the ham bone and salt pork, with water to cover. When the meat is falling off the bone and the peas are well cooked, add the peas and chopped vegetables to the meat and meat broth. Cook all together until done, taking care not to scorch the bottom of the kettle. Before serving, pull the meat from the ham bone and put into the soup. Remove the salt pork. This soup is good the first day and even better the second. 12 generous servings.

GRAVLAKS

This is a supreme snack with a glass of good Danish beer. It has its roots in Norway. For each pound of fresh salmon, use the following:

2 tablespoons sea salt
2 tablespoons sugar
pinch salt peter
handful of spruce twigs
1 teaspoon white peppercorns, coarsely ground
large handful fresh dillweed sprigs

Clean and bone a salmon. Take a large enameled baking dish and line with spruce twigs. Rub the salt, sugar, and salt peter into the salmon. Put the salmon in a dish, skin side down. Sprinkle with pepper and dill. Put the other half of the salmon on top, skin side up. Cover with more dill. Put a weighted chopping board on top of the salmon and put in the icebox for 48 hours. Remove and cut into diagonal strips. Remove the skin. Serve with buttered rye bread.

One of the deeply rooted experiences I've had on this peninsula was a session spent at the Clearing near Ellison Bay in 1955. I was nineteen and by far the youngest member of the class. Mertha Fulkerson was then in charge, a small, quiet-spoken dynamo. We students were a motley bunch of academics, lost souls, and just plain folks.

Jens Jensen's Clearing was then, as now, a retreat of startling beauty, a true clearing place for body and soul. (An Esalan for straights, as a California friend recently said to me.) Although Jensen was a successful landscape architect, he was also a visionary, one who translated those visions into solid reality.

A part of his philosophy for the Clearing was that each person should work on the land. We worked on the stone fences and gathered firewood. I was there to study anthropology, but being there was the essence of the week. The silence seemed palpable. It remains so today. Walking through the woods or sitting above the water in Jensen's stone overlook nourished us as much as the food that came out of the kitchen.

We ate at a common table in the handsome main lodge, lingering over our meals, becoming acquainted in the heat of argument. The food was plain and good. I recall a fruit soup.

NORWEGIAN FRUIT SOUP

1 pound mixed dried apricots, apples, and pears
3 quarts water
¾ cup sugar
½ lemon, juice and grated peel
3 tablespoons cornstarch
pinch salt

Take a good-sized, heavy pan and soak the fruit in water for an hour. Add the sugar, lemon, and salt and bring to a boil. Simmer for at least one hour. Mix the cornstarch with a cup of the juice, stir in, and continue to simmer for another hour. Cool. Serve this soup hot or cold in old-fashioned soup plates with a dollop of sour cream.

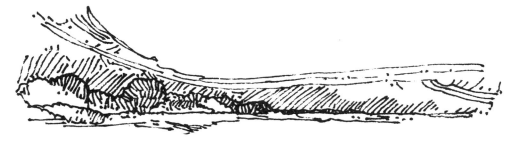

One cold, crisp morning we had Swedish pancakes with lingonberries. These were the same wonderful pancakes that I used to eat at Al Johnson's very early in the morning after staying out all night with a bunch of friends on the beach.

These pancakes are best made in iron crepe pans or plattar pans, which have small indentations for pouring in the batter. There seem to be as many recipes as there are cooks to make the cakes. Experiment until you find a batter that suits you.

SWEDISH PANCAKES

¾ cup sifted flour
½ teaspoon salt
1 teaspoon baking powder
2 tablespoons sugar
2 eggs, separated
1 cup whole milk

Sift the dry ingredients into a bowl; stir in the egg yolks and milk. Beat the whites until stiff and fold in gently. Heat the griddle or pan. Add a little butter to each indentation. Just before the butter starts to smoke, spoon in the batter. Bake over moderate to high heat until the edges curl and bubbles form on the surface. Turn over and cook on the other side. The process takes only a few minutes. Serve hot with lingonberry sauce. This recipe makes about 30 three-inch cakes.

Pancakes for supper go well with the traditional Swedish meatballs.

SWEDISH MEATBALLS

1½ pounds ground beef
½ pound pork steak, ground
1 cup breadcrumbs
salt and white pepper to taste
1 small onion, grated
2 eggs
¼ teaspoon nutmeg
butter

Have the butcher put the meat through his grinder twice. Put the meat in a mixing bowl. Soak the breadcrumbs in water and squeeze out any moisture. Add the crumbs to the meat. Mix in the eggs one at a time. Add the seasonings and mix well, using your hands. Form into small balls. Heat the butter with a bit of oil (to prevent burning) in a heavy skillet. Brown the meatballs on one side, then jiggle them to brown evenly all around. Add enough water to cover them. Cover the skillet and simmer for at least an hour. Serve with pan juices. 6 to 8 servings.

The final rootedness is in the house and the land we live on. Sometimes we are lucky enough when first setting eyes on a place to know we must live there, that we are meant to make it home. This happened to our family with a small house in the woods near the tip of the peninsula.

The house, clapboard over stove wood, was built on a dry stone foundation. When we moved in, it had been propped up in the center, and the edges of the house were splaying out into the garden. It was in danger of not holding together. Slowly, over the years, we have put things to rights. In the process, we discovered a secret passage and some old bones, and I found I had to write a book about that adventure.

In fact, I've written several books in this house, for it is open to any creative effort, whether cooking, painting, or writing. It is plain and spare, and we have kept it that way. The old floors are birch and beech; the beach sand comes in and I sweep it out. The few furnishings are Wisconsin country, picked up at farm auctions and flea markets. The pantry is stuffed with old pots, pans, and utensils bought for spare change.

The kitchen, as with many old houses, was an added improvement, for in its early days all cooking was done in the main room. The new addition is small: it takes a refrigerator, a dough table, a sink, and a stove.

I regret there's not room enough for a wood-burning stove in the small kitchen next to the old electric stove. But I live in the twentieth century, and although I have cooked by necessity on a wood stove in a mountain cabin, to get a fire

hot enough to bake a pie and roast a chicken on a hot summer's day is literally enough to drive a cook out of doors.

    The next recipe, a nineteenth century dessert, is a case in point. The original calls for four hours in a slow oven. Who in the family would want to stick around to feed the stove? No wonder our forebearers often moved their cooking to outdoor lean-tos in midsummer's heat.

APPLES AND PEARS PUDDING

apples
pears
stale bread slices
cinnamon
brown sugar
butter
fruit juice

Butter a deep baking dish. Cover the bottom with bread slices. Layer in sliced apples and pears. Sprinkle with brown sugar and cinnamon. Make alternating layers of the above ingredients until the dish is nearly filled. End with bread slices. Pour in any fruit juice you have handy. Dot with butter and put on a lid. Bake in a 350-degree oven for 1½ hours. Remove and serve hot or cold. This pudding is excellent for breakfast with cream poured over the top.

Wherever I've traveled, I've eaten the local bread and gone home to attempt to duplicate it in my own kitchen. Door County is no exception. Every bakery up here makes a good loaf of limpa, but I had to try it for myself. The following recipe makes a much less refined bread than most bakeries around. Children who've not grown up on it may find this bread "too spicy." You may wish to cut the quantity of flavorings, depending on your family's tastes. But try it first as printed.

LIMPA BREAD

1 cup boiling water
½ cup cracked wheat
1 teaspoon fennel seed, crushed
1 teaspoon ground cumin
1 heaped teaspoon grated orange peel
2 teaspoons salt
⅓ cup molasses
3 tablespoons shortening or lard
1 envelope yeast
¼ cup warm water
1 cup milk
2 cups rye flour
4½ cups unbleached white flour

Take a large dough bowl and put into it the cracked wheat, fennel, cumin, orange peel, salt, molasses, and shortening. Pour over these ingredients a cup of boiling water. While this is cooling, dissolve the yeast in warm water. While the first set of ingredients are still warm, add the yeast mixture. Then add the milk and rye flour and mix. Add the unbleached flour gradually. When you have a workable dough, allow it to rest for a few minutes. Knead for 10 minutes and place in a large, greased bowl. Butter the top and set to rest and rise for approximately 2 hours, until nearly doubled in bulk. Punch down and form into a large round loaf. Place on a greased cookie sheet and allow to rise until nearly doubled again. Bake in a 350-degree oven for an hour and a quarter. Brush the crust with melted butter and cool the bread on a rack. Tastes best with unsalted butter.